AN ARABIAN COLLECTION:

ARTIFACTS FROM

THE

EASTERN PROVINCE

AN ARABIAN COLLECTION:

ARTIFACTS FROM

THE

EASTERN PROVINCE

Grace-Burkholder

AN ARABIAN COLLECTION:
ARTIFACTS FROM THE EASTERN PROVINCE
First published in 1984 by
GB Publications
862 Jeri Lane
Boulder City, NV 89005

©1984 Grace Burkholder

Library of Congress Catalogue Card Number: 84-70783

ISBN: 0-9613535-0-3

Production Graphics/Printing
Graphics West
Las Vegas, Nevada

Technical Supervision by A.F. Herrera
Photography and maps by Grace Burkholder
Drawings by Pat Johnston

iv.

11370

ACKNOWLEDGMENTS

Many people have helped make this volume a reality and I am deeply indebted to them, especially those "early Aramcons" whose enthusiasm for the desert was contagious. Annette Matthews gave so untiringly of her time in the location of reference materials. Geoffrey Bibby first identified the 'Ubaid pottery for us in 1968. Edith Porada guided my first attempts at reporting accurately. S.M. Amin provided many helpful suggestions concerning the photography. Pat Johnston rendered the beautiful drawings. Alicia Geer insisted that I must do a book. Mary Soroka Cashion not only offered continual encouragement but devoted countless hours to the selection and arrangement of the material. My heartfelt thanks are extended to each one.

— GRACE BURKHOLDER

CONTENTS

PLATES

INTRODUCTION

From the rocky plateaus to the hollows nestled between the dunes, from the myriad shell heaps along the coast to the shores of the inland salt flats, from the perimeters of the lush oases to the edge of isolated wells, man has throughout countless millennia left evidence of his continual habitation of the Arabian Peninsula. In the very beginning, that period of prehistory which is slowly becoming better understood, early man roamed the terrain searching out the edible plants and following the game to the watering places. From the widely scattered and relatively modest-sized habitation areas of early man, as defined by the chert implements and debris, it is possible to trace a gradual but continual expansion in population and settlement size extending into modern times.

Arabia has not always been a desert. Recent research indicates that climatic changes included some wet periods in the Arabian Peninsula.[1] Lakes formed in depressions while streams carried seasonal runoff. Man was able to satisfy his essential needs in many areas which today are totally void of surface water.

Distributed along these ancient water sources the early campsites reveal the tools and dibitage of chipped-stone industries by which archaeologists can define subsistance patterns with ever-increasing validity. Large game was more plentiful. Animals which are no longer hunted today, wild goats, gazelle, oryx, onager, ostrich and cheeta contributed to the ecological balance.[2] Petroglyphs pecked into the rock surfaces in many areas (at a much later date) not only depict

---

[1]McClure, Ar Rub' Al Khali, pp. 258-260, documents two wet periods with radiocarbon dating of several lake beds in the Ar Rub' Al Khali, ranging from about 36,000 years B.P. to about 17,000 years B.P. and a later period from about 9,000 years to 6,000 years B.P.

[2]Dickson, pp. 465-466, in writing about the Arabian Peninsula prior to 1949 lists the following animals as common: oryx, gazelle, wild goat, ostrich and cheeta. Harrison, *The Mammals of Arabia*, p. 622, in listing extinct mammals includes the onager.

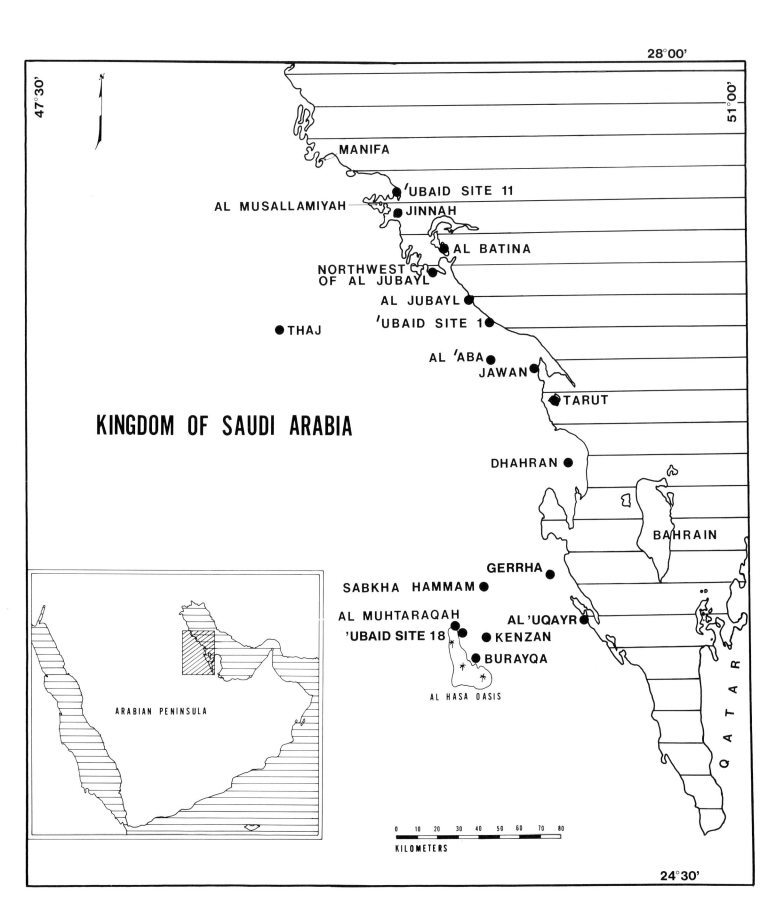

Area Of Investigation
(Sites Mentioned In Text)

many of these animals but show human figures in various activities including hunting scenes where raised spears pierce the game.[3] Some of the earliest tools found in the Arabian Peninsula are the large crude handaxes fashioned from stone or more often readily available chert which was easily fractured conchoidally to provide sharp cutting edges where needed. No doubt more perishable items such as containers for carrying berries and roots, digging sticks and twisted fiber ropes supplemented these stone tools but we can only speculate about their nature at this time as we observe some of the still primitive societies living in the warm climates of Africa and Australia.[4]

Richard Leaky tells us that man's sharing nature contributed to his survival in a competitive world. Instead of eating alone whenever the food was found man carried it "home" and subsequently shared it not only with his children but with his extended family. This daily food-sharing experience kept small groups together and consequently promoted more cultural interaction.[5] Although we are unable to trace language development patterns or other changes in cultural modes we do have fragments of fossilized bone and stone-tool assemblages which are datable in their African context and allow us to formulate hypotheses about these early years not only in the neighboring African homeland but in the Arabian Peninsula as well.

The transition to a more complicated life-style began some 40,000 years ago with the appearance of tools such as burins, backed blades, notched blades and awls by which other tools were fashioned. Long thin blades, indicative of the changes that took place in the tool-making technology, help distinguish these later campsites. Various hypotheses have been offered concerning the introduction of the bow and arrow. The British Museum in a recent report entitled "Man Before Metals" tells us that the earliest direct evidence indicates it

[3]This author has not encountered any petroglyphs in the Eastern Province, but they are found at many locations in the central part of the peninsula. Anati has provided two volumes on *Rock-Art in Central Arabia* with numerous examples cited: Vol. 1, fig. 11, ostrich, fig. 62, large feline, fig. 84a, horned animal and two ostriches, p. 152, classification of animal figures, Vol. 2, Part 1, Pl. X, wild ass, Vol. 2, Part 2, fig. 1, eight ibex.

[4]Leaky, and Lewin, *People of the Lake,* pp. 141-142.

[5]Leaky, and Lewin, *op. cit.,* p. 139.

was used in North Germany ca. 11,000 to 10,000 years ago. Regardless of the date or place this new weapon probably had a greater impact on man's control of his food requirements than any previous invention. Carefully worked arrowheads found at all the later Arabian habitation sites testify to its popularity.

During the fifth and fourth millennia small village sites distinguished by the easily recognized 'Ubaid pottery were established near lakes, artesian wells and inlets from the Gulf.[6] Villages may have existed much earlier, but at this time we have concrete evidence of permanent building materials in the form of reed-impressed plaster found at four coastal sites. The introduction of trade with other areas is also documented. Small boats made their way between the coastal villages bringing the hard-fired decorated Mesopotamian pottery to the Eastern Province in exchange for the pearls gathered in the Gulf waters. From as far away as Lake Van, Anatolia, come a few blades and small obsidian beads.[7] The origin of this volcanic glass has been established through its trace-element analysis.

Dr. Abdullah Masry, Assistant Deputy Minister of Education for Cultural Affairs, devoted his thesis in 1972/73 to a study of the interregional interaction patterns in Northeastern Arabia. Sondages were excavated at three sites which had painted 'Ubaid sherds amongst the surface debris. Dr. Masry tells us that it was highly possible that interregional interaction was developing before the 'Ubaid period as nomadic peoples contacted each other and the exchange of raw materials ensued.[8]

---

[6]The discovery of painted Ubaid sherds in Saudi Arabia in March, 1968, was made by this author. It is documented by Bibby, *Looking for Dilmun*, p. 376, and *Preliminary Survey in East Arabia 1968*, p. 64, and reported by Burkholder, Ubaid Sites and Pottery in Saudi Arabia.

[7]Colin Rendrew commented in a personal communication, dated March 8, 1974, on obsidian samples from an Arabian Ubaid site and other samples from south of Dhahran. "…..the analyses clearly suggest that all the obsidian in use in the Persian Gulf was from east Anatolia (VAA) origin. Dhahran is 1500 km. from Lake Van, and this is the greatest distance from the original natural source recorded for any obsidian finds in the Old World."

[8]Masry, *Prehistory in Northeastern Arabia: The Problem of Interregional Interaction*, p. 183, "From the same perspective, the prehistoric evidence from northeastern Arabia offered in this study clearly establishes this area as a major focus of interrelationships involved in the Ubaid configuration. A pristine cultural tradition was seen to have existed here prior to the development of material-culture parallels (primarily consisting of painted pottery) with Mesopotamia. Perhaps interregional contacts were already underway well before the time of the appearance of the first pottery."

4

Following the 'Ubaid period and extending through the third and second millennia the villages became substantially larger and the sites are more frequently encountered.[9] The inconspicuous local-made pottery of this period too long has been ignored. Numerous inland sites of significant importance, showing close parallels with each other in pottery fabrics and shapes, have filled a gap which was heretofore left void. Attention meanwhile has centered on the small port of Tarut which has produced one of the finest single collections of carved steatite in the known world.[10] Now steatite is not found in the geological formations of the Eastern Province which causes one immediately to pose a question concerning its origin. Directly eastward across the Gulf at Tepe Yahya, Lamberg-Karlovsky reports on the steatite workshops excavated there and their proximity to ancient mining areas.[11] The Zargos Mountains where steatite is a common occurrence are one possible source while Oman or the Buraimi Oasis have been suggested as other possibilities. Trace element analysis will eventually help to identify the sources of the Tarut steatite. The important issue remains that as early as the third millennium a vast network of maritime activity was evident in Gulf waters linking the major sites with each other and with coastal Arabia.[12]

During Hellenistic times the entire Eastern Province was bustling with activity. Fortifications testify to the need for security from within.[13] The remains of villages and small cities dot the countryside.

---

[9]This author read a paper on one of these sites at the Seventy-fifth General Meeting of the Archaeological Institute of America held in St. Louis, Mo., Dec., 1973. The site is described in detail in this volume under the section entitled "Sabkha Hammam."

[10]Burkholder, Steatite Carvings from Saudi Arabia, describes some of the major pieces in this collection.

[11]Lamberg-Karlovsky, *Excavations at Tepe Yahya, Iran*, p. 61.

[12]Porada, Some Results of the Third International Conference on Asian Archaeology in Bahrain, March 1970: New Discoveries in the Persian/Arabian Gulf States and Relations with Artifacts from Countries of the Ancient Near East, Introductory Remarks, p. 294, published in *Atribus Asiae* XXXIII. Lamberg-Karlovsky, Tepe Yahya 1971, Mesopotamia and the Indo-Iranian Borderlands, p. 99, also contributes to this topic.

[13]Bibby, *Preliminary Survey in East Arabia 1968*, pp. 10-14 and 43, investigated Thaj, a fortified Hellenistic city dating roughly 300 B.C. to 100 A.D. The city wall was quadrilateral in shape, 4.4 meters thick, built of squared limestone blocks facing both sides of a rubble core. Square towers were evident at two corners. Bibby also reports on forts in a location he refers to as "the irrigation area." He describes a "sabkha fort" measuring about fifty meters on each side and an "inland fort" measuring fifty-two by forty-nine meters.

The entire region enjoyed the prosperity fostered mainly by the importance of the trade in frankincense. With its origin hidden away on the mountain slopes of the southern Arabian coastal areas and certain places along the African coast the gummed excretion of the frankincense tree became a valuable trade item. It was highly prized for its medicinal and votive properties on the alters of the Mesopotamian and Mediterranean world. Complementing this was the fact that Arabian seamen held the carefully guarded secret of the alternating northeast and southwest monsoon travel across the Gulf to India, sailing east in the summer months with the aid of the southwest monsoon and utilizing the northeast monsoon on their return trip in December or January. Trade in gold and ivory from the African coast along with the spices from India helped to classify the Arabian entrepreneurs amongst the richest people in the known world.[14]

The formidable deserts not only isolated the peninsula but at the same time protected it from exploitation by its northern neighbors. However after the trade secrets were discovered this good fortune did not last. Power passed from one country to another and the contest for the control of Gulf shipping supremacy continues even today.

Following on the heels of the Hellenistic period Arabian sites display a wide variety of sherds which may be classified as Sassanian. Most popular are the eye-catching blue-green lead glazes which are found in abundance in many areas. It is doubtful if any of these glazed vessels were locally made. Even today in the markets of Qatif one can find two products similar in appearance but from different locations: the Qatif-made jugs and bowls and identical-appearing ones imported from Basra. The merchants charge more for the Basra vessels but are quick to recommend them because they are made from finer clays.

With the coming of Islam vital changes were generated throughout the entire Middle East. Superior craftsmanship and new discoveries are evident in many fields. In keeping with this impelling force, as

[14]In his article, Frankincense and Myrrh, pp. 78-80 and 88, Van Beek provides a wealth of information concerning the locations where frankincense and myrrh were obtained, the land and sea trade routes, the uses and the cultural impact on the area.

early as the eighth century and widespread by the ninth century, tin-glaze techniques were developed by the Islamic potters working with the excellent river clays found around Baghdad and Samarra.[15] Introduced at this time was the method of lustre painting which created a metallic sheen on the glazed ware giving it the illusion of having been painted with gold.[16] Fragments of exquisite tin-glazed vessels have been found in the coastal areas of the Eastern Province from Manifa to Al Uqayr. Fishing/pearling activities were a vital part of the subsistance pattern of the many villages which were located adjacent to the Gulf waters. Sizable areas strewn with sherds often with ancient fish weirs still intact nearby offer their silent testimony.

Early Islamic sites often include sherds of the hard-fired Celadon imports from China. This pale green pottery was very popular from the tenth century on until it was finally replaced by the Ming imports (second half of the 14th century) found at some sites, mainly Tarut, Jinnah and Al Musallamiyah.

During the early Islamic period glass vessels made their appearance in the Eastern Province. Now glazes, a prerunner of glass, were used as early as 4000 B.C. in Egypt and Mesopotamia to coat steatite and quartz beads, but the hollow glass vessels date only to ca. 1500 B.C. in Egypt. During the second millennium cuneiform tablets testify to glass terminology in Mesopotamia. During Roman times glass cutting and blowing became further refined.[17] However glass is conspicuouly absent from Thaj, a large Hellenistic site, and it is not until early Islamic times that we find fragments with beautiful patina on them scattered amongst the Islamic sherds.

It is fortunate for the archaeologist that internment customs during the 'Ubaid period through the Sassanian period provided for the ritual of food and other accompaniments for the deceased. Most of the

---

[15]Lane, *Early Islamic Pottery,* p. 13.

[16]Lane, *op. cit.,* pp. 14-15.

[17]Displays in the British Museum of Natural History, London, depict the history of glass from its earliest beginnings. Lane, *Early Islamic Pottery,* p. 8, tells us about the earliest use of glazes in Egypt. *Ancient Glass in the Freer Gallery of Art,* published by The Smithsonian Institution in 1962, depicts many lovely glass vessels which date to the second half of Dynasty XVIII (ca. 1430-1340 B.C.).

artifacts recovered from Tarut fall into this category. Consequently today we are aware of parallels in style and material that would otherwise be lost if these vessels had not been thus preserved. Archaeologists are now equipped to collect a vast store of information from habitation sites through the use of a multi-disciplinary approach. One technique is the flotation process which separates plant remains from soil samples. It is not unusual to recover charred seeds which can be isolated and tabulated helping to identify food products, wild and cultivated, from any given strata of the excavation. Geological investigations help to establish changes in climate, water sources, sea levels and pinpoint available mineral deposits. Dating procedures include both Carbon 14 determinations and Thermoluminescence for the more recent finds and may employ Potassium-aragon analysis or Archaeomagnetism for earlier dates. Catchment-basin studies help to determine the environmental impact upon a site and help identify the resources available to its inhabitants.

Cultural studies may also be employed to identify spatial patterning of land utilization. The identification of bone fragments recovered in an excavation assists with zoological aspects of the environment and may be helpful in determining if the animals were wild or domesticated. The study of artifacts, however interesting they may be, is only a small part of the archaeological search for man's history on earth.

In a volume such as this there is no possible way to include all the localities where stone tools may be found or where pottery lies on the surface. However by selecting a few representative sites, some of which are limited in their span of occupation, data can be assembled that should prove most useful to the comprehensive picture. The material included here, collected from the Eastern Province of Saudi Arabia, offers a keyhole introduction to the historical importance of this area.

The earliest periods of human habitation throughout the Arabian Peninsula are still a matter of inference and speculation. Terminology such as paleolithic and mesolithic is meaningless without supportive evidence and certainly cannot be attached to random surface finds. Styles of workmanship, i.e. Acheulean, should refer only to similar techniques and not imply any correlation with dated materials from other locations. Due to the fact that only limited excavation has been permitted within the Kingdom, and because analytical methods of dating chipped stone are still in the developmental process, it is difficult to present a scientific approach to the prehistoric periods. Many of the reported sites are merely thick deposits on a totally wind-eroded surface. Many others invite careful excavation. Arabia is indeed an archaeological wonderland.

ARCHÆOLOGICAL SITES

AL MUHTARAQAH
25°38′ North Lat.   49°35′ East Long.

Beyond the modest village of Al Muhtaraqah, which lies at the northernmost end of the Al Hasa oasis barchan dunes slowly encroach on the stretches of salt flat. On the eastern perimeter of this low drainage area several small mounds rise only perceptibly above the otherwise flat terrain. To the casual eye they are barely worth investigation for no striking features command attention. It is one of these small gravel-covered rises measuring less than 500 meters from north to south and about 200 meters from east to west which offers a single facet through which we can begin to comprehend prehistoric man in the Arabian Peninsula.

Scattered over the southeastern edge of the mound are the tools and debitage of a blade-oriented workshop. Beautiful combinations of rusts, tans and browns streak and mottle the chert. Scanning the ground for pottery produces no results, for this is truly an aceramic site. Absent also are the large handaxes of earlier years or the large hand-held grinding stones associated with later village life. The long blades, mostly the debris of the industry, lie in profusion. Some are questionable implements in as much as they display no secondary retouch, but others qualify as beautifully worked points (Plates 4a, 4e, and 5a). Mixed with the long blades are delicately worked arrowheads (Plates 5c and 6b).

This small area is similar to many of the flint sites mentioned in the somewhat sparse literature concerning the archaeology of the Arabian Peninsula. Henry Field has very appropriately collected and listed locations for us. More recently Abdullah Masry excavated comparable material at a site only a few kilometers to the S.E. of Al Muhtaraqah.

An examination of the faunal fragments recovered from level 12a of that excavation suggests that a predominance of large mammals, onager or wild half-ass (Equus hemionus or Equus asinus) were associated with the site at its lower levels. Level 9 provided a C14 determination of 7060±445 B.P. (5110 B.C.) Libby half life 5570 years. Obviously a hunting/gathering economy sustained early man at this and similar sites.

Comparable flint sites, found in Africa and Eurasia, range from a beginning some 40,000 years ago and continue until the transition to village life. This change probably occurred sometime during the sixth or fifth millennia in Eastern Arabia. Caution should be exercised here that we are not overinclined to theoretically place all the sites at the older end of this era. Robert Braidwood explains this time span very adequately for us. At the beginning of this period tools fashioned for the purpose of making other tools appear on the scene. This represented considerable advancement from the handax-oriented technique that had prevailed for over a million years. Jacquetta Hawkes suggests that this breakthrough may have been promoted by the increased use of language, the development of coherent speech. Whatever the cause we can only speculate about it at this time.

However, our knowledge of man's early beginnings has been considerably extended during the past decade as archaeologists delved into ancient gravels and penetrated rock shelters and caves. The Arabian Peninsula with vast areas still awaiting exploration is slowing gaining recognition as a likely center of paleolithic activity comparable to the surrounding areas which stretch from Africa to the steppes of northern Iraq and Iran.

Geological studies by Harold McClure in a report on ancient lake beds in Rub' Al Khali confirm geographical changes which have taken place over the past thirty millennia and provide evidence for two very wet periods, an early one dating from 36,000 to 17,000 and a later one centered around 7,400 Before Present. It has become increasingly apparent that hunting/gathering activities by Homo sapiens around the ancient lake beds were more than an occasional occurrence.

The Arabian Peninsula is well represented by sites where the blade-tool technique predominated. Because this manner of tool production continued basically unchanged for such a long period of time many more Arabian sites need to be examined before we can reach relevant conclusions.

AL 'ABA
26°44′ North Lat. 49°45′ East Long.

Another flint site which should be included here has an entirely different appearance. It rests high on the eastern slope of a large rocky limestone outcrop. The site overlooks an artesian well which provides for the small oasis at the base. The worked stone appears to cover a much longer time span than that at Al Muhtaraqah and displays considerably more variety. The large stone handax shown in Plate 2, with a portion of the cortex still remaining, fits perfectly in the right hand. It is typical of the large crude all-purpose implements early man needed for grubbing, cutting, pounding and scraping. The blade tradition is represented by a number of long thin blades (Plate 3c).

However the most significant implements found here are the tile flint knives and scrapers which lie in abundance on the hillside. This variety is a natural phenomenon in this area. In many places around the large Sabkha Edh Dhabiya, located just ten kilometers south of Al 'Aba, the ground is a mass of tile flint which has collected on the wind-eroded surface. A few smaller areas covered with the thin slabs are within easy walking distance of Al 'Aba.

Holger Kapel, in writing about discoveries in Qatar, classifies the implements as knives if they are worked on both dorsal and ventral faces and as scrapers if the retouch is confined to one surface. These tiles became very popular during the 'Ubaid period as evidenced by the hundreds found on the Arabian 'Ubaid sites. Crude little arrowheads, with the white crust still intact on both faces, were often worked from the thinner slabs. Here at Al 'Aba the tile flint implements, both knives and arrowheads, seem to be in a totally aceramic context. Whether they preceded or were contemporary with the 'Ubaid period has not been determined.

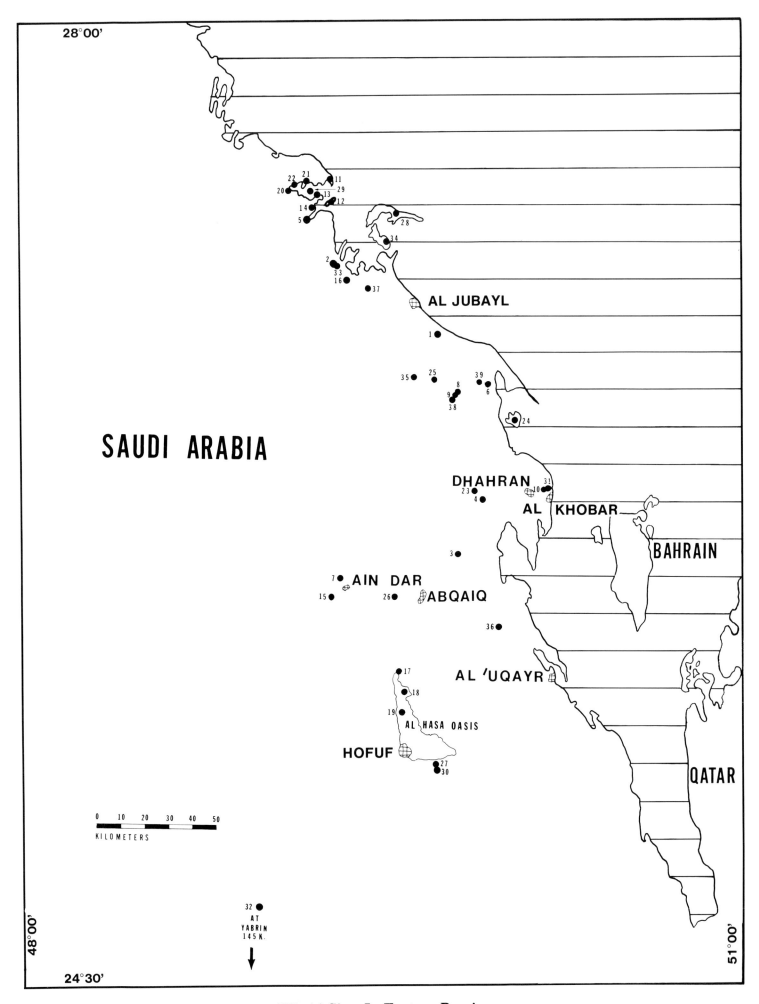

28°00'

22 21
20   11
      29
   13
14   12
5

2
33
16   37

1

AL JUBAYL

35   25   3 9
      8   6
   9
   38

24

SAUDI ARABIA

DHAHRAN   31
23   10
4

AL KHOBAR

BAHRAIN

3

7 AIN DAR
15   26   ABQAIQ

36

17   AL 'UQAYR
18
19
AL HASA OASIS
HOFUF
27
30

QATAR

0 10 20 30 40 50
KILOMETERS

32
AT
YABRIN
145 K.

48°00'

24°30'

51°00'

'Ubaid Sites In Eastern Province

'UBAID SITES

After the initial discovery of 'Ubaid pottery in the Eastern Province in March, 1968, additional sites were found so that by the spring of 1972, thirty-nine locations had been recorded. Some of these sites constituted a single painted sherd in a jumble of pottery and flint representing many periods. Others were obviously habitation sites with remnants of building materials in the form of reed-impressed plaster. Some sites were coastal at present-day sea level, others were over sixty-five kilometers inland. Sites were numbered for easy identification by the order in which they were found. When it is recalled that the 'Ubaid culture, blanketing southern Mesopotamia in the fifth and early fourth millennia, represented mankind's first concrete development in what has been defined as civilization, the historical impact of finding the pottery as far away as eastern Arabia can be readily understood.

The research of the intervening period has helped fill in some of the pertinent data. It is now generally accepted that the painted 'Ubaid pottery had its origins in northern Mesopotamia and the technique then spread southward as the rapidly-developing agricultural-based economy insured the survival of a much larger percentage of the very young and the very old. Pottery was certainly an asset to a settled population; even today nomads never carry anything so fragile, but prefer skins and old inner tubes for milk and water. To date, the limited archaeological investigations of the Arabian Peninsula have located no pottery types predating the 'Ubaid ware.

On the Arabian sites the hard-fired painted ceramic, unmistakable criterion of this culture, ranges in thickness from two millimeters to over two centimeters, and in color from buff to yellow green (Plate 7 and 9c). Variations in matt paint from dark brown to black are most likely due to variations in the firing temperatures. Paint is most often applied in geometric designs on the exterior upper portions of jugs and deep bowls and on the interior surfaces of shallow dishes. Designs include stripes, both thick and thin, wavy lines, scallops, lozenges,

17

triangles, chevrons, zig-zags, ladders and circles along with nets and stylized fish, birds, trees and flowers. A number of sherds are solid black on one surface, patterned on the other. Sometimes the designs are in reserve. A few vessels are slipped but more often the paint is applied in bold strokes directly to the surface.

Over a dozen different rims styles with many minor variations were immediately evident at Site 1. Vessels seemed for the most part to have been round-bottomed, for ring bases along with spouts were most uncommon. Only a few handles of the horizontally-pierced lug type were found. A considerable number of rims with an inner ledge designed to hold a lid, had holes pierced before firing presumably for lid attachment.

An undecorated, hard-fired reddish paste is sometimes also present. Another ceramic type which is found in abundance on a number of the Arabian sites is a very coarse red ware with copious amounts of straw temper (Plate 9b). This ware frequently shows signs of burning particularly on the lower sections of the vessels and often has protruding knobs to facilitate handling over a fire. It obviously represents the everyday cookware while it is just possible that the finer highly-prized ceramic may have been primarily reserved for votive and internment accompaniment.

The colorful chert on most of the Arabian 'Ubaid sites represents the debris of flake oriented workshops. Frequently the ground is strewn with waste flakes and cores. Numerous tile flint knives and scrapers along with crude tanged and barbed arrowheads are usually present. Some of these points are so small as to indicate they might have been designed for fowling.

All the evidence to date seems to point to the fact that trade routes between Mesopotamia and eastern Arabia were well established during this period. The 'Ubaid ware, fired to a temperature comparable to the requirements for stoneware (over 1000° C.) was a particularly durable product and was therefore easily imported in quantity by small craft coming south to such locations as our Site 1 (Dosariyah) where surface sherds numbered in the tens of thousands, and subsequently found its way inland to a number of villages. A negative item to be sure, but important none the less, is the fact that there have been no kiln wasters found on any Arabian 'Ubaid sites. Imports from as far away as Anatolia included a small quantity of obsidian in the form of blades and small disk-shaped beads. Grain was also a most likely import. Several stone querns from Site 1 and Site 11 bear testimony to this hypothesis. In exchange it can be assumed pearls were a major export item. The coastal sites have provided a large number of miniature flint awls, many less than two centimeters in total length, that have no explainable use other than drilling holes in pearls (Plate 9a). The large heaps of oyster shell associated with these awls would substantiate this theory.

At Eridu, a prominent site in southern Mesopotamia, the 'Ubaid culture was closely connected with maritime activity; a clay model of a sailboat was excavated from a grave and fish offerings were found in a temple. The major Arabian sites are oriented around lakes, artesian wells and inlets from the Gulf. Many of these former inlets have now become salt flats, only a few meters above present-day sea level, as the wind-driven sand has settled and filled them over the centuries.

The farther south and inland we search, the less pottery we are able to locate on the surface. Many of the more southern flint sites which appear to be both pre and post 'Ubaid by the analysis of the surface sherds and the lithic technology, have thus far not revealed a single painted fragment. The Al Hasa oasis, supplying a quantity of fresh water and being the source of the best present-day potter's clay, would seem the logical place for a concentration of 'Ubaid pottery if Arabia were ever more than the peripheral limits of this pottery style. But instead, Al Hasa has thus far produced only sites with a few scattered sherds. The evidence from Site 18, Ain Qannas, close to a lake bed, indicates a limited number of vessels. Joan Oates, in commenting about a prominent vessel, a large shallow bowl decorated on the interior with oblique hatching and on the exterior with reserve triangles, tells us that it cannot be assigned definitely to any period earlier than 'Ubaid 3. Most of the sherds of this single vessel, riddled with mend holes, were collected from the surface around a small nuclear mound rather than on it. The oval outline of the mound itself appeared to be a very powdery soil consisting of thoroughly decomposed vegetation resembling ashes. The surrounding area about 1.5 meters lower than the mound and comparable to level 4 of the major sondage excavated by Abdullah Masry in 1972, was strewn with flint debris and pottery of many different periods. It contained 'Ubaid sherds from only five different vessels, one of which was the easily recognized 'eggshell' also attributed to 'Ubaid 3.

The earliest temple architecture, excavated at Eridu by Seton Lloyd and Fuad Safer, was a combination of mud brick and reeds sometimes plastered on both sides with clay. The reed-impressed plaster found in Arabia on four coastal sites provides an interesting parallel demonstrating a somewhat advanced technology. Strangely enough at two sites over 70 kilometers apart barnacles were found attached to the flat sides of chunks of this building material. In both locations the barnacle encrusted pieces were located over four meters above present-day sea level. No logical explanation for this has been presented. A sea-level rise of over four meters, remaining high for the several months it would require for barnacles to attach and grow, seems not only improbable but is not documented by additional evidence from other Arabian locations. Since several 'Ubaid sites are at present-day sea level it seems unlikely that a gradual uplifting of the land mass along the eastern seaboard could have occurred since 'Ubaid times. It might just be that large plastered containers, perhaps sunken into the earth and refilled regularly with sea water, would provide a unique way of keeping seafood alive and protected from sea birds and thus edible in a warm climate. This, of course, is only a hypothesis, as neither buildings nor containers have been found.

What is most urgently needed is a thorough excavation of some of the known sites particularly those which suggest by surface materials that they might provide a sequence from 'Ubaid into Uruk or later periods. Unfortunately several are already being swallowed by advancing urbanization. Mounds are being flattened to provide fill for new roadways while commercial structures are encroaching upon others.

TARUT
26°34′ North Lat. 50°04′ East Long.

The tiny island of Tarut, measuring just six kilometers from north to south and three and one-half kilometers from east to west, which has provoked many questions among today's scholars, may someday provide us with significant information concerning developments in the Gulf.

At the southernmost end of the island the fishing/pearling port of Darin occupies a vantage point along the main navigable water approaches to the very shallow bay. The town stands prominent on the horizon and spreads over the southern peninsula which appears to be a sprawling tell five meters above the low palm-canopied gardens. An old fort overlooks the harbor where small craft unload their wares today just as they might have in ancient times. For this island with its bountiful artesian wells close to the shore affords the sweetest and most easily obtainable water of any port on the Arabian coast. Since the coastal area north of Manifa has very limited water today, it can be logically conjectured that supplies of fresh water would have been a controlling factory there in former times. No wonder then that sailing ships stopped at Tarut to take on water, dates, wool, salt, hides and other precious cargo. In exchange during the late fourth and early third millennia they brought the handsome stone vessels of carved steatite and translucent marble which keep turning up on Tarut as today's gardeners cultivate and expand their gardens (Plates 10, 13, 16a, 16b, 16c, 21a, and 27b). Still later magnificent vessels of the Akkadian and Hellenistic periods proclaim the continued prosperity enjoyed by the inhabitants of Tarut (Plates 33, 40a, 40b, 41c, 45c, and 46b).

At the northern end of the island just west of Zor several huge mounds of burned earth mixed with fish bones suggest a sizable settlement. Ming sherds and black bracelet pieces can be seen on the surface. A short distance inland, but still along this northern shore, complete Barbar vessels have been recovered along with others displaying the fine red ware and black paint of the Umm an Nar pottery (Plates 17 and 32c).

Mention should be made here of the eye-catching fort on the island's central tell made immortal by Geoffrey Bibby's description in "Looking for Dilmun". Overlooking the women's private bathing area located around one of the large artesian wells, stand the ruins of a Turkish fort which afford a panoramic view of the gardens. Barbar sherds seen around the base have excited considerable speculation concerning what the lower levels may reveal.

SABKHA HAMMAM
25°46′ North Lat.   49°42′ East Long.

Over a thousand rock tumuli on a high limestone plateau overlook a salt flat where a busy salt-mining operation is located today. Who were these people? When did they live? Why were they all buried here in this desolate area? Did they mine salt at this spot in ancient times?

Closer examination reveals that most of the tumuli have been opened at some time. In most cases the upper rocks have been thrown aside to permit entry from the top. Around the base of some of these mounds the scattered fragments of broken pottery can be seen, almost as if these bits had been discarded when the graves were disturbed. Frequently these sherds are of a red paste and often they have been highly burnished (Plate 24c). Others retain evidence of black paint which seems to have been applied on the entire exterior surface or in a band below the rim. Around several of the tumuli long tubular ceramic beads were found. They are crude in appearance, so highly fired as to be almost vitrifed (Plate 24b).

It was the impressive tumuli field that prompted an investigation, but data concerning the geographical changes in the Eastern Province and the discovery of a prehistoric habitation site along an ancient watercourse soon became a vital link.

When considering the geography of the surrounding area we find that the Al Hasa oasis, largest in the Kingdom of Saudi Arabia, lies just over fifty kilometers from the Arabian Gulf. The one hundred eighty square kilometers of gardens were fed until recently by sixty major springs. A few years ago thirty of these springs were incorporated into the massive Al Hasa Irrigation and Drainage Project, a tremendous undertaking designed to more than double the area of cultivation. Surface and underground channels leading to two huge evaporation areas, north and east of the oasis, provided the necessary drainage. Just north and slightly east of the northern evaporation sea Sabkha Hammam is located.

Somehow these huge evaporation seas were inadequate to cope

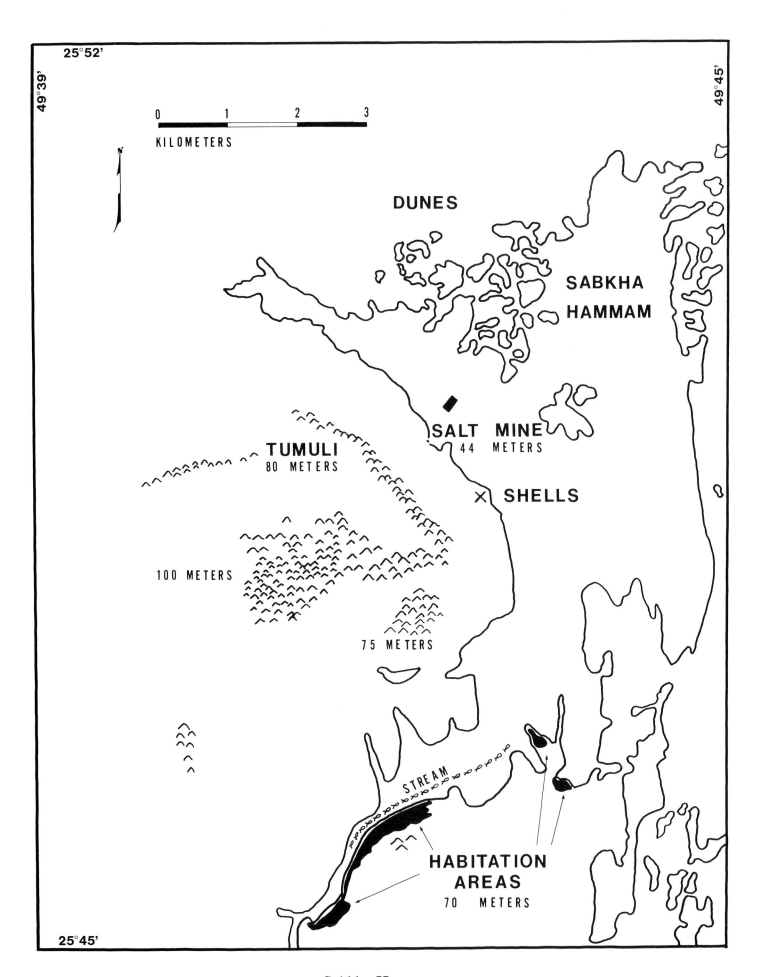

Sabkha Hammam

with the initial quantity of water that poured into them and a small channel made its way through the dunes to the coast fifty kilometers distant. New fresh-water lakes were formed in the low depressions. Vegetation is already springing up around these newly formed lakes inviting the return of migratory birds and game in an otherwise hostile environment.

Now the Al Hasa gardens have an average elevation of 140 meters. In prehistoric times, when the water supply was much larger, the overflow found its way eastward to the coast just as it does today. As one explores the vast area of enormous dunes between the oasis and the Gulf, fresh water snail shells can be observed as a carpet in many areas, clear proof that quantities of fresh water existed there in ancient times.

Further research in the area has brought forth some remarkable discoveries. Some of the ancient underground channels have been reactivated by this new drainage project, and it is one of these that we want to discuss here. The map (page 26) provides a closer look at Sabkha Hammam. The tumuli field is located along the rocky area on the western ledge. The mounds are concentrated in a southern cluster, an enormous central group and a line stretching along the edge of the plateau in addition to peripheral scatterings. Until recently this salt flat was considered to be a continental sabkha, that is, it had no visible water flowing either in or out. The nearest water supply would have been the Al Hasa oasis over eighteen kilometers away. The seepage water, thought to come from the surrounding dunes had such a high salinity that a vast reserve of salt was available for the mining operation on the northwestern edge of the basin.

But now along the southern shore a small stream comes to the surface and flows approximately three kilometers from west to east before it disappears into the sand. This water is more than a simple seepage product for the stream is filled with small fresh-water fish, a type classified as Aphanias dispar, which frequent the warm springs of the oasis.

Even more remarkable, at the spot where this small stream erupts is an ancient habitation site with pottery that not only matches the pottery of the tumuli area, but belongs to the early third millennium B.C.

From a prehistoric standpoint the site is particularly large, measuring over three kilometers in length it stretches in a narrow band along the salt flat edge. Numerous outlines of walls, houses and stone channels can be observed. Several of these channels measure over eighty meters in length and are arranged perpendicular to the edge of the salt flat suggesting that an erosion control project might have existed here several millennia ago. The deep gullies which cut through the site would help to validate this theory. Some areas display evidence of massive burning.

The pottery, spread in quantity on the surface, is drab in appearance, frequently it is a red paste with black paint. Some sherds have a cream slip decorated with a red paint. All are badly weathered. Many pieces indicate that they belong to large globular bowls. A few are obviously from collared jugs. No spouts are evident but flat bottoms are not uncommon. There is no overlay of later cultures.

The site is scattered with flint tools and the waste flakes of the industry. Arrowheads include a variety of types not only in the material selected but in the style of execution. The tile flint scrapers found so frequently with the 'Ubaid culture are the exceptional examples on this site. A few scraps of copper/bronze can be seen amongst the sherds but the large amount of flint indicates that metal was still a scarce commodity in this community. A tubular ceramic bead, similar to those from the tumuli area, and two polished shell beads were found. Most interesting were the serrated flint saws lacking any evidence of siliceous gloss, but which might have been used for cutting reeds along the water's edge.

It seems only reasonable to suggest that this salt flat was a fresh-water lake at the time the village was occupied for all around the western edge the ground was covered with the shells of fresh-water snails, a type classified by the British Museum as Melania tuberculata Muller. Some of these shells were gathered from a spot about one meter above the present salt flat level and sent for a radiocarbon analysis. The date obtained was 2495 B.C. ± 95 years which when converted for the known variation in radiocarbon determinations in the third millenium gives us a corrected date on the Masca scale of 3010 to 3110 B.C.

In summary, a large early chalcolithic site extended along the shore of a sizable fresh-water lake. The geographic changes which eliminated the water may very well have terminated the habitation at this site. As far as it is known there existed a simple village life dependent upon an abundance of waterfowl and game. A few copper/bronze scraps provide limited evidence of trade connections.

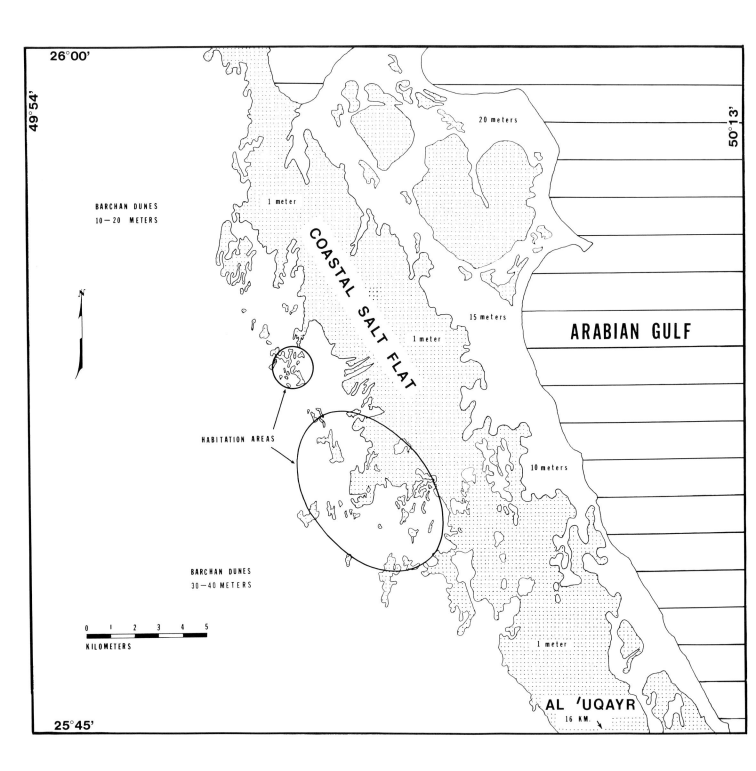

26°00'

49°54'

50°13'

BARCHAN DUNES
10—20 METERS

20 meters

1 meter

COASTAL SALT FLAT

15 meters

1 meter

ARABIAN GULF

HABITATION AREAS

10 meters

BARCHAN DUNES
30—40 METERS

0   1   2   3   4   5
KILOMETERS

1 meter

AL 'UQAYR
16 KM.

25°45'

Gerrha

GERRHA
25°50′ North Lat.   50°02′ East Long.

Twenty-five kilometers northwest of the port of Al 'Uqayr where the coastal salt flat meets the dunes, a vast network of ancient irrigation channels can be more easily traced on the aerial photography than on the ground. These salt-encrusted aquaducts, appearing to have no visible water source such as lakes or wells, lie in parallel lines with their western ends hidden by the encroaching white sand. The most acceptable explanation is to assume that the overflow from the artesian wells of Al Hasa, in the form of a small river, supplied the water for this area, and the aquaducts were constructed merely to control local distribution. In this deflation area the channels, now slightly raised, imply that perhaps a half meter to a meter of soil has blown away in the interim.

Scattered over the site which encompasses several square kilometers, the remains of small villages and two strategically placed rectangular forts can be identified. From this locality which local people have suggested as the long-lost city of Gerrha come the beautiful beads pictured in Plate 42. Carnelian, cut in a variety of shapes predominates, but rock crystal, amethyst, shell and beautifully polished stones are well represented.

The surface pottery (Plate 35b and 38a) belongs primarily in the Hellenistic period with a suggestion of earlier ware in the northern areas where a few Jamdat Nasr type rims can be seen. Here also are the remains of another rectangular fort, much more impressive than those in the southern section, built of stone rubble measuring around 80 meters east to west and 110 meters north to south. On the northern side the thick walls, approximately 1.4 meters, are clearly delineated by parallel rows of stones while in other places they seem to be a mass of fallen rubble. These walls are still over two meters high in the southwest corner. In addition to the fort there are several small mounds upon which foundations remain intact. The immediate vicinity has a supporting area of irrigation outlines similar to those farther south. It was from this northern area that a frit seal was found several years ago and later identified by the British Museum as Jamdat Nasr. From the south several cylindrical seals not only help date the ruins but testify to commercial activity with foreign ports. Quantities of small irregular lumps of copper have been found on the surface along with corroded bronze points (Plate 35) common during this period. It should be noted here that the great quantity of copper scrap implies a wasteful culture with many copper/bronze implements.

Now the classical geographers, mainly Strabo, Pliny and Polybius basically describe Gerrha as being five miles in circumference, having towers and houses made of salt, and lying on a deep sinus or bay. Fifty Roman miles (38 miles) inland was the third district of the Gerrhaei "Attene" a rather poor district but villages and towers had been established in it for the convenience of the Gerrhaei who cultivated it. Equidistant from the shore was the island of Tyros (generally identified as Bahrain) extremely famous for its numerous pearls. The magnificent wealth of the Gerrhaei, chiefly a product of the carefully guarded frankincense trade, allowed them to possess a vast equipment of both gold and silver articles such as couches and tripods and bowls together with drinking vessels and very costly houses; for the doors and walls and ceilings were varigated with ivory and gold and set with precious stones. No wonder then that we continue to search for this lost city.

Our location certainly seems to fulfill the requirements of the classical geographers. Since no stone was available locally buildings might easily have been constructed of blocks of salt mud cut from the nearby salt flats. The surface of such buildings would soon have become salt encrusted giving them the appearance of towers of salt. It takes little imagination when looking at the map (page 30) with its wide costal salt flat, now less than two meters above sea level in many places, to see how this easily might have been, 2500 years ago, an extension of the present-day inlet north of Al 'Uqayr. Thus the location is ideal, equidistant from Bahrain and the gardens of Al Hasa (Attene). Not only is there the necessary Hellenistic pottery on sites on the eastern side of the Al Hasa gardens at Jebel Burayqa and Jebel Kenzan to satisfy the description of Attene, but Bilbana, which Ptolemy's geographic material indicates was located on the coast approximately ninety-five kilometers north of Gerrha, can then be identified as present-day Jawan.

Over the years local amateur archaeologists have collected a wealth of material from this site: beads, seals, gold earrings, etc., all more durable artifacts than the pottery, much of which seems to have badly disintegrated by the alternate dampening and drying year after year in the highly saline mud. Additional habitation areas no doubt extended into the sabkha on the eastern perimeter. The outline of one fort has been traced far out in this vast salt flat where the irrigation channels lose their identity. Other pottery strewn depressions lie to the west midst the encroaching dunes.

Even as Gerrha ceases to exist in the literature after the beginning of the Christian area, this site has no indication of later habitation.

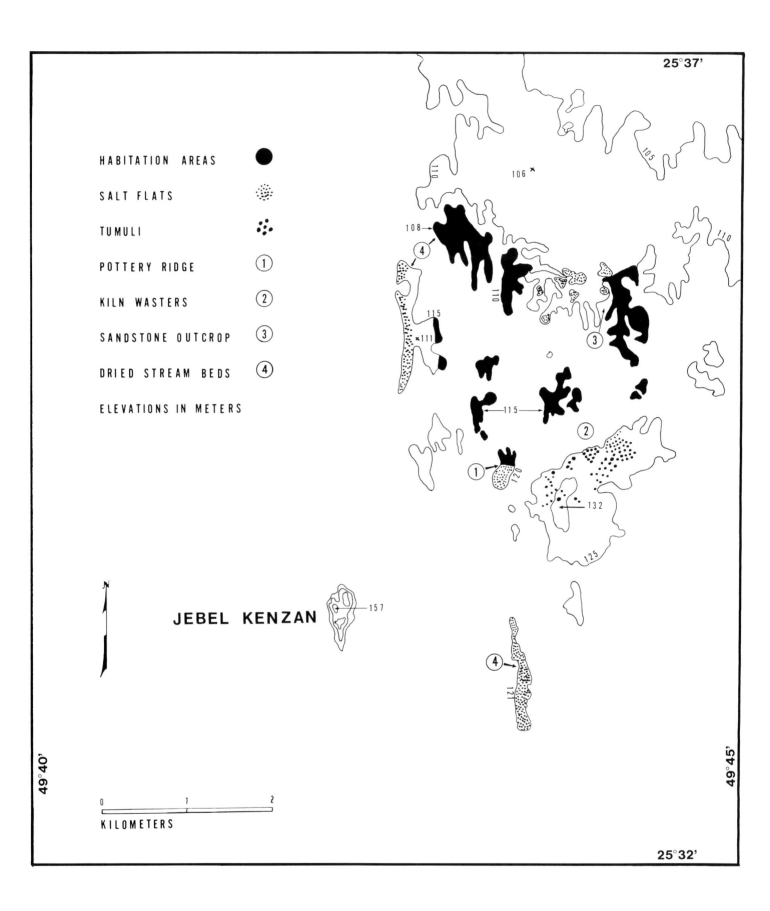

HABITATION AREAS

SALT FLATS

TUMULI

POTTERY RIDGE ①

KILN WASTERS ②

SANDSTONE OUTCROP ③

DRIED STREAM BEDS ④

ELEVATIONS IN METERS

JEBEL KENZAN

25°37'

106 ×

105

110

110

108→ ④

110

115

×111

③

④ ①

115

②

120

132

125

157

④ 121

49°40'

49°45'

0   1   2

KILOMETERS

25°32'

Jebel Kenzan

KENZAN
25°35′ North Lat.   49°44′ East Long.

Jebel Kenzan, a limestone outcrop twenty-three kilometers N.E. of Hofuf lends its name to a nearby achaeological site which affords a new perspective in the literature of this area.

Nestled between massive barchan dunes, several square kilometers lie cluttered with potsherds dating to the Hellenistic period. Shifting sands act as a dererrent in establishing an exact size for this site, but quantities of broken pottery extend over an area measuring approximately three kilometers north to south and two and one-half kilometers east to west. Interspaced are several small sibak (sabkhà, singular) suggesting that small fresh water lakes may have been present here in ancient times. Today these sibak are low flat areas with a thick crust on a salty mud base. They are quite treacherous to drive upon, particularly after a rain.

One such sabkha near the southwestern perimeter of this site has a ridge extending in an east/west line almost across it. This ridge, about three meters wide and approximately one-half kilometer long is thickly strewn with broken pottery. Many of the sherds are from very large vessels; some are kiln wasters. It is possible that this ridge served as a low bulkhead, either to prevent flooding of adjacent habitation areas, or to provide control over the fresh water stream which interlaced the site. The dried bed of this stream can be seen a short distance to the south. The exposed section is around five hundred meters long, running generally in a north/south direction. The channel itself is about three meters wide and is lined with fresh-water snail shells, tuberculata Muller. Smaller sections of similar dried stream beds can be found along the western edge of the habitation site.

Another interesting feature is a reddish sandstone outcrop which overlooks a salt flat in the northeast section. On its flat summit a rectangle approximately ten by eleven meters suggests the remnant outline of a building.

Rather centrally located is a peculiar spot that reminds one of the area around a kiln. Absent is the huge mound of pottery you would expect to find, but scattered over the blackened ground are a considerable number of misshapen kiln wasters and baked lumps of clay, some clinging to small rocks. Material of this sort is often used locally today to seal the upper chamber of a kiln when firing is in progress. A large sand dune is superimposed on this area. Perhaps it conceals the actual kiln. Two unaccountable circles about two meters in diameter can be seen in another hollow. Except for the above mentioned phenomena the habitation areas are void of foundations or distinctive features. In some places the ground is hard and dark and appears to have been burned. In other areas the surface is wind eroded. The site is unencumbered by the remains of later periods.

Of particular concern is the raised gravel plain which lies adjacent to the site on the southeast. Along the edge of this gravel formation over fifty earth-covered tumuli ranging in height from one to three meters can be seen. At first they appear to be a natural phenomenon such as one would expect to find when a raised area has eroded gullies along its escarpment face. Closer examination contradicts this assumption, for the mounds are definitely higher than the level of the plateau and are formed in regular circles. Nearby depressions suggest where gravel may have been removed to form some of the larger tumuli. Most interesting are five pieces of cut limestone blocks which lie scattered amongst the mounds and would lead one to believe that at least some of graves contain well-formed chambers. One such stone, cut on five faces, lying exposed in the central area measured 44 by 30 by 26 centimeters. Another seen on top of a mound a short distance to the east, cut on only three faces, measured 54 by 28 by 21 centimeters.

The use of cut limestone blocks in the Eastern Province during Hellenistic times has been documented by F.S. Vidal in his excavation at Jawan and by Geoffrey Bibby at Thaj. It is not unusual then that cut stone should be present at Kenzan and it would seem most appropriate that it would be used in forming grave chambers for the more elaborate burials. Incidentally no cut stone was observed in the habitation areas. Now the Eastern Province has tumuli, both rock and earth covered, in many locations. As would be expected, most tumuli indicate by their irregular crowns that they have been the subject of investigation over the centuries. It seems most improbable that the Kenzan tumuli would have escaped notice, unless by their very nature of appearing to be part of the escarpment face, they were considered natural. With few exceptions there is no evidence to indicate that they have been subjected to plundering.

Three copper coins plus a silver coin that had been cut in half lay amid the habitation debris. They are very similar to the coins found at Thaj which are slightly concave disks bearing the representation of the seated figure of Zeus. One of the copper Kenzan coins and the silver half-coin were still in good condition and showed such an imprint on the concave surface when they were cleaned. The reverse sides were undecorated. One electrum (?) bead was found. It is very nearly circular, .7 cm. in diameter with a rather large hole.

Like most Hellenistic pottery found in the Eastern Province, the Kenzan assemblage is not particularly impressive. A variety of vessel shapes can be observed. Most common are shallow bowls, many of which have a shaved lower edge and a small flat bottom. A few have the short tripod legs that were popular during this period. A considerable number of huge storage jars are evident. Handles are rare but one small lug type was noted. No spouts were found. An occasional piece of light gray steatite in the form of a bowl fragment should be mentioned here.

The pottery is most often red with sand tempering, however gray smother-fired wares and greenish grays are also abundant. Some of the gray bowls have a solid black painted exterior or a solid red wash. Also found were vessels of red paste with a cream slip. Glazed sherds were noticeably absent.

Kenzan certainly warrants a more thorough investigation. Unlike Thaj, which lies 150 kilometers to the northwest and which probably postdates Kenzan and Gerrha, it has no broken terracotta figurines scattered on the surface, no scraps of "attic ware", no alabaster nor rocker incised designs (Plate 45). Unlike Gerrha, about forty kilometers to the northeast (23 miles) Kenzan has no abundance of beads or copper scraps strewn about. However it seems to compare favorably with the description offered by the classical geographers, Pliny and Polybius when writing about Attene, inland district belonging to the Gerrhaei.

JAWAN
26°42′ North Lat.   49°58′ East Long.

On the western side of Tarut Bay two kilometers of low salt flat separate the water from the magnificent tell known as Jawan crowned with Islamic sherds and coins. The rubble of buildings protrudes from a deep cut made by a bulldozer when quarrying rock to build a refinery was a mandatory operation years ago. F.S. Vidal and Donald Holm, under the auspices of the Saudi Arabian Government early in the 1950's, excavated a sizable mound which was threatened with destruction from nearby blasting, to reveal a cruciform chamber of cut stone dating to the first century A.D. That this tell was a busy site during Hellenistic times is evidenced by the countless sherds in a deep red carpet on the exposed hilltops. Around the base worked flint bespeaks of an earlier habitation.

Richard LeBaron Bowen Jr., describes this tell quite appropriately as a necropolis, for a considerable number of graves, sometimes as cists cut into the solid rockbed, sometimes as earth covered mounds, are still apparent. From the southern slopes come the two exquisite earrings which were lying exposed on the surface as the hillside eroded away (Plates 44a and 45b).

Hellenistic and Islamic sherds are not confined to this tell alone for Jawan is surrounded by similar areas. On the mound adjacent to the north in the same coastal salt flat quantities of Hellenistic pottery can be found exposed on the hilltop and the northwestern slopes. High in the dunes to the west one can not only observe pottery but also stone foundations which imply an extensive area of habitation. At the highest elevation the land mass to the south of Jawan reveals a rectangular enclosure not precisely compass oriented but measuring approximately thirty-five meters along each side. The walls are of limestone rubble about seventy-five centimeters thick. Pottery of mixed periods and fragments of very weathered marine shell and flint cover a substantial area.

Perhaps Jawan with its adjacent settlements will someday be

identified as Bilbana, the coastal town shown on Ptolomy's maps. It would seem that Jawan and Thaj continued to prosper after Gerrha's decline. With the death of Epiphanos (164 B.C.) when Babylonia became part of the Parthian Empire, caravan routes between Sabaea and Nabataea replaced much of the former commerce up and down the Gulf. This would help explain the predominate rocker design, popular on Parthian pottery, and repeated on many vessels at Jawan and Thaj, but noticeably absent at Gerrha and Kenzan.

NORTHWEST OF AL JUBAYL
27°07′ North Lat.   49°28′ East Long.

In the excitement generated by prehistoric sites the numerous Islamic settlements which flourished on the Arabian mainland are apt to be overlooked. So thick are the sherds it is difficult to attempt any separation of the locations. All along the coast in the area from Manifa to Al Uqayr the beautiful glazes of the Islamic potter can be found in quantity.

One site of particular interest which should be included here because it furnishes material for comparative analysis lies on the coast twenty kilometers northwest of Al Jubayl. Habitation debris extends for approximately three kilometers along the shore in an area protected from the open sea by islands. Adjacent to the present-day tide line are two sprawling hills separated by a low drainage channel. The northern windswept slopes are a mass of stone rubble wherein the outlines of buildings are plainly discernable. The stone, known as farush, is a conglomerate of limestone with much imbedded shell and can be collected easily along the shoreline in many places.

One building of farush close to the western end measures three and one-half by eight meters. The walls formed by a double row of stones are approximately one half meter wide. Close by is a large rectangular enclosure measuring 36 meters east to west and 31 meters north to south. Here the walls are thicker, about 80 centimeters, with straight sides as carefully arranged as rough stones would permit. On the south side a peculiar pile rubble extends into the enclosure as if it might have been a fallen structure or gateway. Several other stone foundations can be seen, however since the number is limited it would appear that these buildings were the more important structures and that the villagers themselves may have erected reed hunts or have lived in tents.

The area covered with broken pottery and glass affords us an excellent early Islamic site of limited occupation. Prevalent are the lovely blue-green glazed sherds in a variety of shapes from small

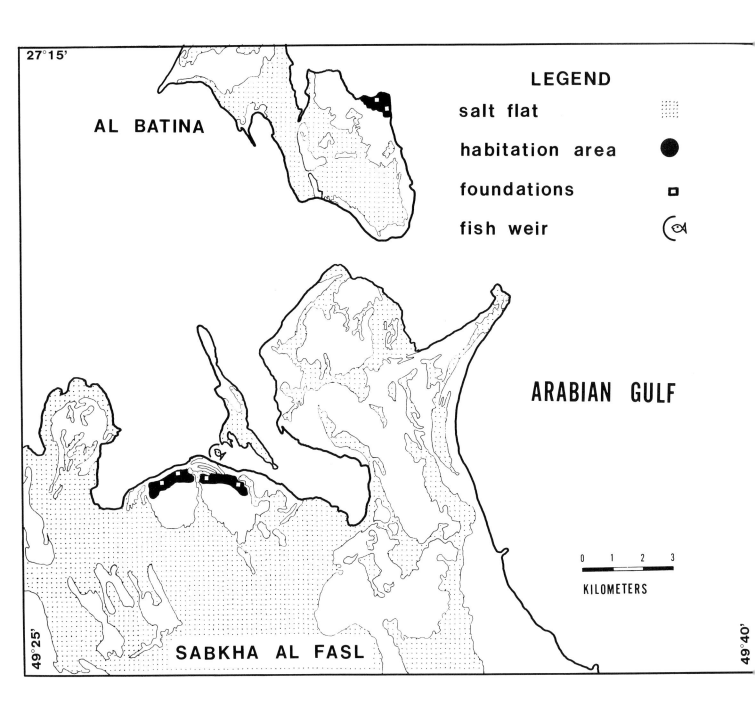

Northwest of Al Jubayl

bowls to large storage vessels. Some display the easily recognized barbotine decoration which incorporates ribbons, any of a variety of rosettes, and usually a rocker design carried over from the Parthian period (Plate 57c). Others with the same glaze have a striking appearance with deeply cut designs which consequently weaken the vessel (Plate 54).

Also present in great quantities is a ware exhibiting a rosy-gray glaze over which the prominent decorations are applied in cobalt, black, aqua and green. The shape of many of these vessels, assigned to the ninth and tenth centuries, influenced considerably by the Chinese simplicity of form, is that of a deep straight-sided bowl. A sharp carination is placed low on the sides, while a delicate ring base finishes the bottom (Plates 61a, 61b, 61c, and 61d). All surfaces are glazed while the simple design without form, in keeping with the teachings of Islam, is reserved for the exterior above the carination.

Another favorite is the more shallow receptacle with a lovely "s" profile. On these bowls which more nearly match Mesopotamian wares, the designs are applied to the interior (Plate 58c). Simple shallow bowls usually with a ring base complement the others (Plate 60c).

A popular parallel is the small molded bowl with a delicate design impressed on the exterior sides and sometimes also on the bottom before a green glaze was applied (Plate 57a). Examination of dozens of sherds indicates no exact repetition of pattern although the bowl sizes are quite uniform. The paste is of two varieties, a salmon and a red, both finely levigated.

Occasionally we find the striking multicolored sherds which compare very favorably with Mesopotamian ninth and tenth century lustreware (Plates 58a and 58b). Habitation seems to have ended shortly thereafter for the site offers nothing postdating the exquisite celadon of the Sung Dynasty.

At this interesting spot beautiful paper-thin blue glass bottles were popular. Their delicate form, usually globular with a long narrow neck, contrasts so sharply with the massive crude green glass fragments which cover the site that it seems almost incongruous that they should be found together. Big cylindrical pieces of glass with a small central hole, too large and crude to be beads, are abundant. Fragments of miniature glass bottles are present (Plate 59) but glass bracelets are conspicuously absent.

The shallow waters of this bay area were condusive to fishing as evidenced by the lengthy stone fish weirs which extend across a narrow channel at the east end. Until recently some of the fishermen in the Eastern Province still used this method of erecting a net on vertical poles pushed into the wet sand. The central stave of the palm frond was particularly adaptable and readily available for this use. After the poles had been pushed into the sand the lower edge of the net was then secured by stones which had been placed along the route beforehand. It was quite a chore for much of the work has to be done in waist-deep water while the tide was in. As the tide receded the fish became entangled.

The economy of this coastal site must certainly be linked with the even larger area of similar Islamic pottery to be observed on the northeastern shore of the neighboring island of Al Batina. One would suspect that pearling was involved but there is no evidence to substantiate this theory. However the pottery, most likely an imported item from the areas around Baghdad, would imply that the community had some export items to exchange. Today the hinterland supports little except the nomadic way of life. Incidentally, no Islamic coins were found on this site. It may be that barter was still the most convenient method of exchange at this early date and that the regular use of coinage was a later development here.

In the rapidly expanding perimeters of Al Jubayl as a modern industrial complex, excavation of sites such as this is highly recommended before it too is leveled by bulldozers to make way for progress.

JINNAH ISLAND
27°22′ North Lat. 49°18′ East Long.

Another interesting Islamic site is situated on an island close to the mainland about 140 kilometers northwest of Dhahran. On the northern end of Jinnah there can be seen an area of shell heaps adjacent to picturesque ruins. South of these huge shell mounds which are the by-product of the thriving pearl industry of yesteryear lies a large area strewn with Ming pottery accompanied by red cookpots with a wide rippled rim extending outward from the vessel (Plate 64c). Here also are black bracelet fragments and noteworthy sherds of a gray or red stoneware with brown glaze.

This site suggests a date for the introduction of the black bracelets which are found so frequently in a totally mixed assemblage. That there were no aqua or multicolored fragments at this specific location is a most significant factor. For the literature is remarkably uninformative concerning these glass bracelets which appear in the Eastern Province in a wide variety of colors: solid black; aqua; brick red decorated with yellow; green and blue stripes; and multicolored combinations (Plate 65). For the most part the bracelets are a smooth band of opaque glass, but a few have been twisted to give an interesting rope effect. The delightful tinkling when several are worn together is, of course, lost but the beautiful fragments continue to satisfy the need for adornment. Local people who have searched diligently for a few bracelet pieces have then had jewelers reset the sections with links of gold so that once again proudly they may be worn.

PLATES

1. HANDAXES
  Cream-colored chert

2. *HANDAX*
   Chert
   Length 11.3 cm.

3. *IMPLEMENTS*
Flint/Chert

4. POINTS
   Flint/Chert
a. *Tan and rose-brown chert*
   Length 3.9 cm.
b. *Striped honey-colored chert*
   Length 5.8 cm.

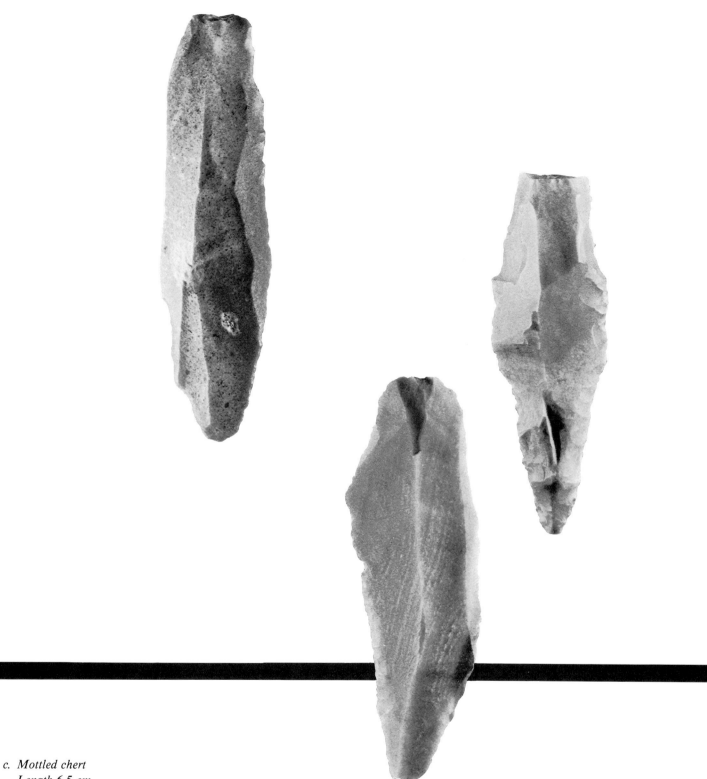

c. Mottled chert
    Length 6.5 cm.
d. Light to medium brown chert
    Length 4.4 cm.
e. Good quality medium brown chert
    Length 3.4 cm.

5. *POINTS*
   Flint/chert
a. *Light brown flint*
   Length 3.8 cm.
b. *Light brown chert*
   Length 3.5 cm.
c. *Light brown flint*
   Length 4.3 cm.
d. *Medium brown flint*
   Length 3.6 cm.
e. *Light orange flint*
   Length 2.5 cm.

6. POINTS
   Flint/Chert
a. *Light brown flint*
   Length 3.8 cm.
b. *Brown streaked chert of poor quality*
   Length 5.4 cm.

7. *BEAKER*
   Black mat paint on yellow-green paste
   'Ubaid 3 period
   End of sixth millennium B.C.
   Height 10.1 cm.

8. BEAKER
(See Pl. 7)

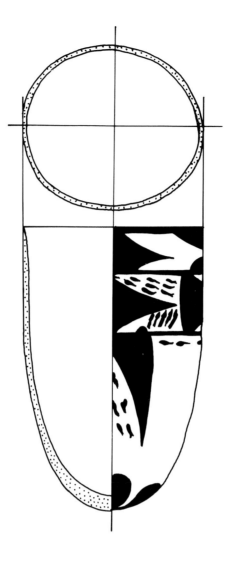

9c. *JUG*
   Black paint, cream slip on a red paste
   'Ubaid Period
   Early fifth millennium B.C.
   Height 26 cm.

9a. *AWL*
   Light orange flint
   'Ubaid Period
   ca. 5000 B.C.

9b. *BOWL*
   Straw-tempered buff paste
   'Ubaid Period
   Fifth millennium B.C.
   Height 16.3 cm.

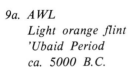

10. VASE
   Light gray steatite
   Proto-Dynastic Period
   End of the fourth millennium B.C.
   Height 11.5 cm.

11. *VASE*
    (See Pl. 10)

12. SPOUTED JUG
    Traces of black paint on a gray paste
    Light colored temper
    Protoliterate Period
    Late fourth to early third millennium B.C.
    Height 22.2 cm.

13. BOWL
    Light gray steatite
    Proto-Dynastic Period
    End of the fourth millennium B.C.
    Height 7 cm.

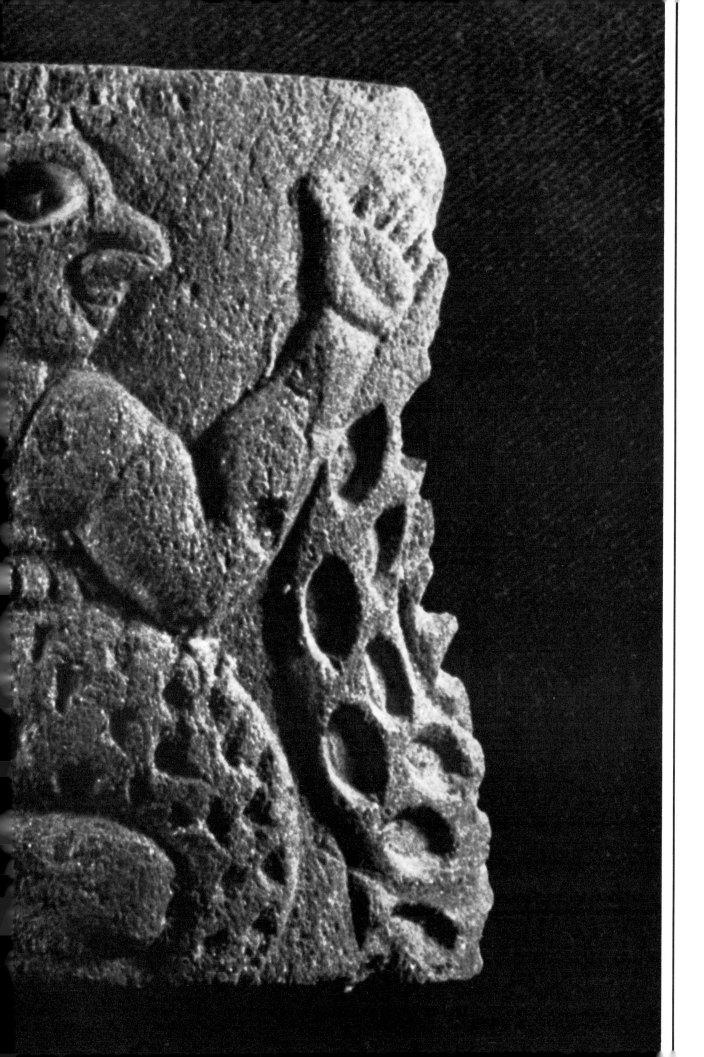

14. *CUPS*
    Left: cream slip on beige paste
    Center: cream slip on red paste
    Right: cream slip on beige paste
    Height ca. 14 cm.

15a. BOWL
Dark gray serpentine
Early Dynastic Period
First half of the third
millennium B.C.
Height 5.8 cm.

15b. ANIMAL FIGURINE
Red paste
End of the fourth millennium B.C.
Height 3 cm.

15c. BEAKER
Cream slip on red paste
Pre-Barbar Period
Early third millennium B.C.
Height 7.5 cm.

15d. BOWL
Light gray steatite
Height 7.1 cm.

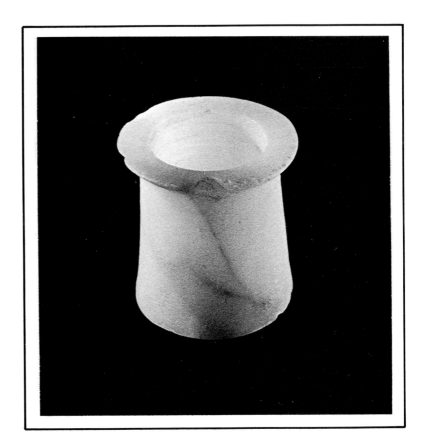

16a. *MINIATURE VASE*
   Travertine marble
   Early third millennium B.C.
   Height 4.8 cm.

16b. *BOWL*
   Translucent marble with
      copper-colored veins
   Proto-Dynastic Period
   End of the fourth millennium B.C.
   Diameter 9.7 cm.

17a. JAR
Buff paste
Jamdat Nasr Period
End of fourth to early third millennium B.C.
Height 20.5 cm.

17b. JAR
Black paint, cream slip on red paste
Umm an Nar Period
Second quarter of the third millennium B.C.
Height 19.5 cm.

16c. BOWL
Translucent marble with copper-colored veins
Proto-Dynastic Period
Diameter 10.9 cm.

18a. *BOWL*
  Translucent marble
  Jamdat Nasr Period
  End of fourth to early third millennium B.C.
  Height 11.9 cm.

18b. *BOWL*
  Dary gray serpentine
  Early Dynastic Period
  First half of the third millennium B.C.
  Height 5 cm.

18c. *BOWL*
  Banded marble
  Early Dynastic Period
  First half of the third millennium B.C.
  Height 3.5 cm.

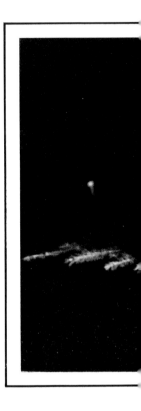

19a. BOWL
   Light gray steatite
   First half of the third
      millennium B.C.
   Height 4.7 cm.

19b. BOWL
   Light gray steatite
   Jamdat Nasr Period
   End of fourth to early third
      millennium B.C.
   Height 7.9 cm.

19c. VASE
   Light gray steatite
   Jamdat Nasr Period
   End of fourth to early third
      millennium B.C.
   Height 12 cm.

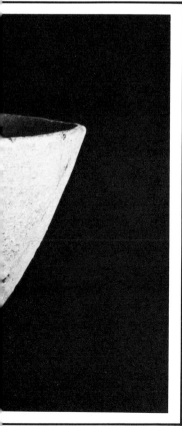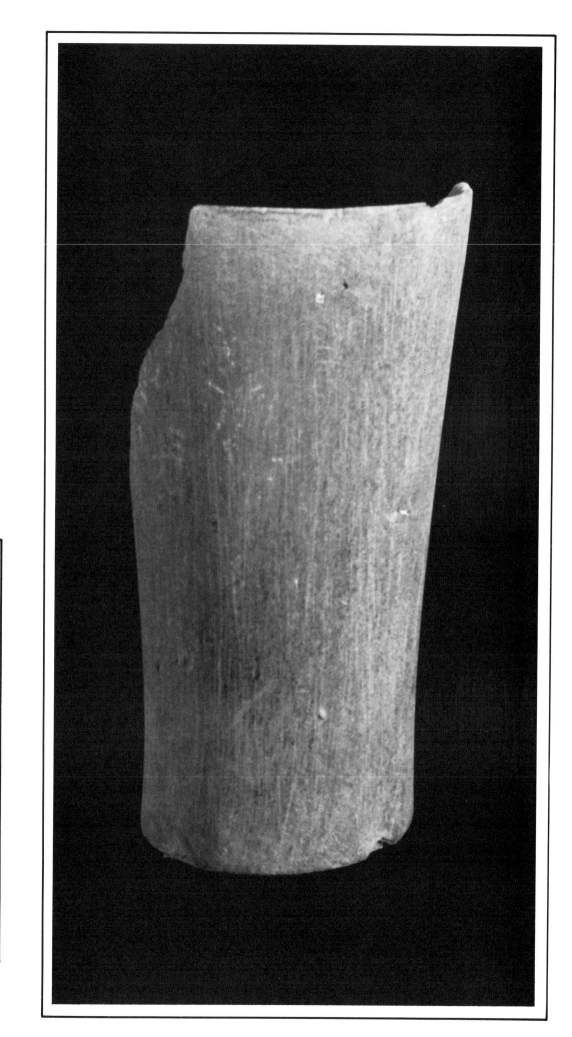

20a. MINIATURE BOWLS
Coarse cream paste
Early second millennium B.C.
Diameter ca. 9 cm.

20b. BOWL
Light gray steatite
Jamdat Nasr Period
End of fourth to early third millennium B.C.
Height 15 cm.

21a. BEAKER
    Argillaceous limestone with coral inclusions
    Early third millennium B.C.
    Height 8.8 cm.

21b. MACEHEAD
    Marble
    Early Dynastic Period
    First half of the third millennium B.C.
    Diameter 6 cm.

22c. BOWL
Light gray steatite
First half of the third millennium B.C.
Height 10 cm.

22a. MIRROR
Copper/bronze
Length 11.5 cm.

22b. COPPER/BRONZE POINTS
Largest one 30 cm.

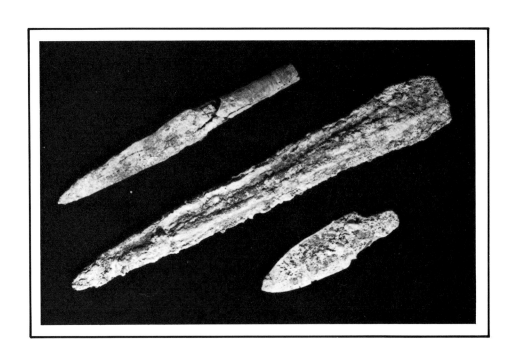

23. BOWL FRAGMENTS
Iron-stained muscovite schist
Early Dynastic Period
First half of the third millennium B.C.
Height 15.4 cm.

24a. *BEAD*
  Shell
  Early third millennium B.C.
  Maximum diameter ca. 2.5 cm.

24b. *BEADS*
  Ceramic, red paste
  Early third millennium B.C.
  Length ca. 3.5 cm.

24c. *JUG*
  Red paste
  Early third millennium B.C.
  Height 16.5 cm.

25. *MINATURE VESSEL*
   Polished light gray steatite
   First half of the third millennium B.C.
   Height 4.2 cm.

26. *GLOBULAR BOWL*
Water-smoothed exterior on reddish-buff paste
Early third millennium B.C.
Maximum diameter 15.3 cm.

27a. BOWL FRAGMENT
Light gray steatite
Early third millennium B.C.
Height ca. 13.5 cm.
Diameter ca. 25 cm.

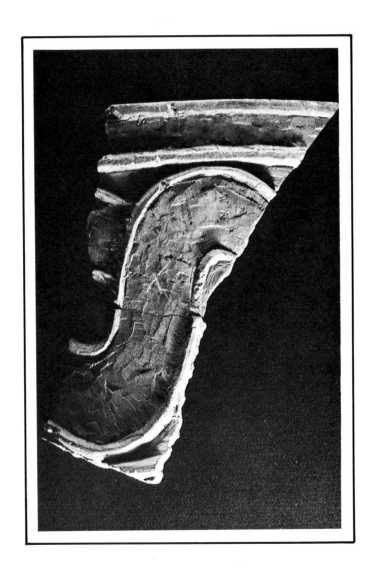

27b. SMALL JAR
   Polished light gray steatite
   Early Dynastic Period II or III
   Middle of the third millennium B.C.
   Height 7.7 cm.

28a. BOWL
Light gray steatite
First half of the third millennium B.C.
Height 9 cm.

28b. JAR WITH BOWL
    Jar: burnished red paste
    Bowl: buff paste
    Early Dynastic Period
    First half of the third
        millennium B.C.
    Diameter of jar rim 12 cm.

28c. MINIATURE SPOUTED
        VESSEL
    Cream slip on red paste
    Larsa Period
    Early second millennium B.C.
    Height 8.7 cm.

29a. *VASE*
     Travertine marble
     Early Dynastic Period
     Height 29 cm.

29b. *SPOUTED JUG FRAGMENT*
     Cream slip on buff paste
     Early Dynastic Period
     First half of the third millennium B.C.
     Diameter of rim ca. 13 cm.

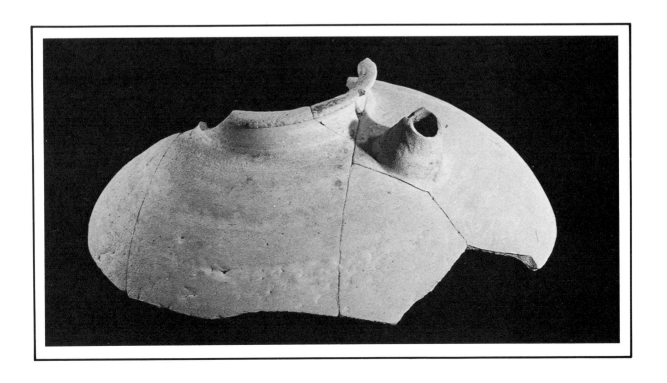

29c. *INCENSE BURNER*
   Light gray steatite
   Early first millennium B.C.
   Height 6.5 cm.

30. JAR
Black mat paint on yellow-green paste
Last half of the third millennium B.C.
Height 16 cm.

31. JAR
  (See Pl. 30)

32a. *SEAL*
   Light gray steatite
   Barbar Period
   Late third millennium B.C.
   Diameter 2.1 cm.

32b. *STORAGE VESSEL FRAGMENTS*
   Cream slip on red paste
   Barbar Period
   Late third millennium B.C.
   Left: diameter of rim 9.2 cm.
   Right: diameter of rim ca. 11.5 cm.

32c. *JUG*
   Red paste speckled with yellow
   Barbar Period
   Late third millennium B.C.
   Height 17 cm.

33. *JUG*
   Red paint, cream slip on buff paste
   Akkadian Period
   Third quarter of third millennium B.C.
   Height 17 cm.

34a. LIMESTONE SHEEP
Height 6.5 cm.

34b. LION SCULPTURE
Limestone
Height 16.8 cm.

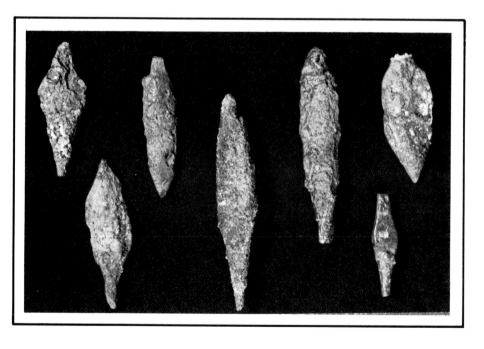

35a. JUG
   Burnished red paste
   Hellenistic Period
   Seventh to third century B.C.
   Height 21 cm.

35b. BOWL
   Red wash on olive green paste
   Hellenistic Period
   Seventh to third century B.C.
   Height 6.7 cm.

35c. COPPER/BRONZE POINTS
   Hellenistic Period
   Seventh century B.C. to first
      century A.D.
   Longest specimen 6 cm.

36a. *JUG*
  Cream slip on red paste
  Hellenistic Period
  Seventh century B.C.
  Height 20.5 cm.

36b. *MINIATURE JUG*
  Red wash on buff paste
  Selucid Period
  Third to first century B.C.
  Height 4.7 cm.

36c. *BOWL*
  Gray finish on a red paste
  Hellenistic Period
  Height 4.6 cm.

37. *SCULPTURE*
Limestone
Height 50 cm.

38a. *JUG*
Greenish-gray paste
Hellenistic Period
Seventh to third century B.C.
Height 21 cm.

38b. *MINIATURE BOWL*
Bright red slip on red paste
Third century B.C. to seventh century A.D.
Height 5.5 cm.

38c. *BOWL*
Beige paste with a brownish patina
Hellenistic Period
Third Century B.C.
Height 4.8 cm.

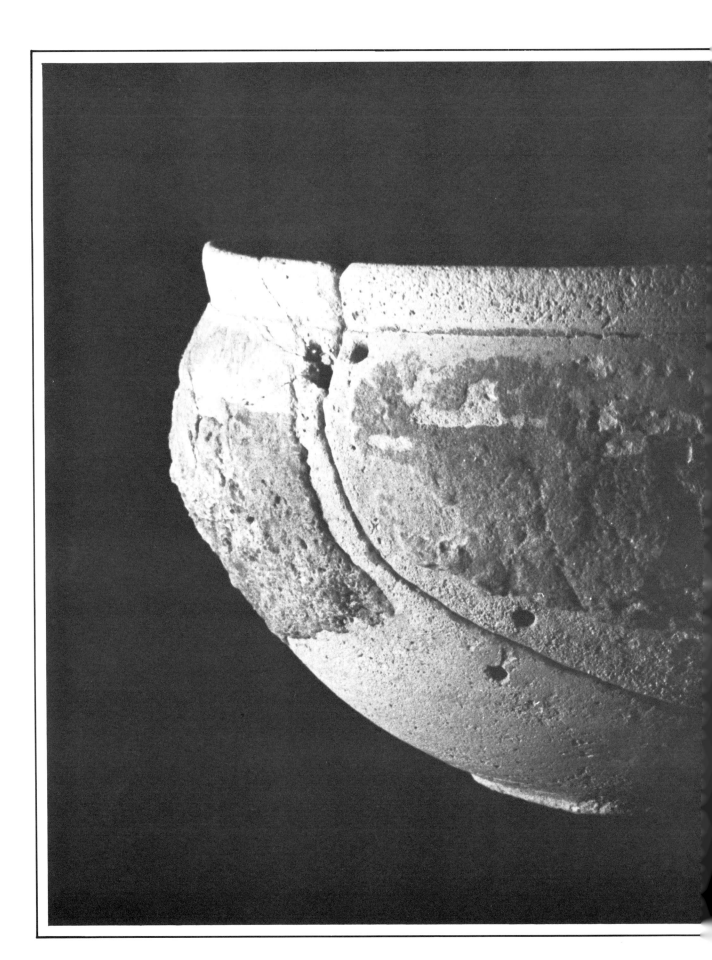

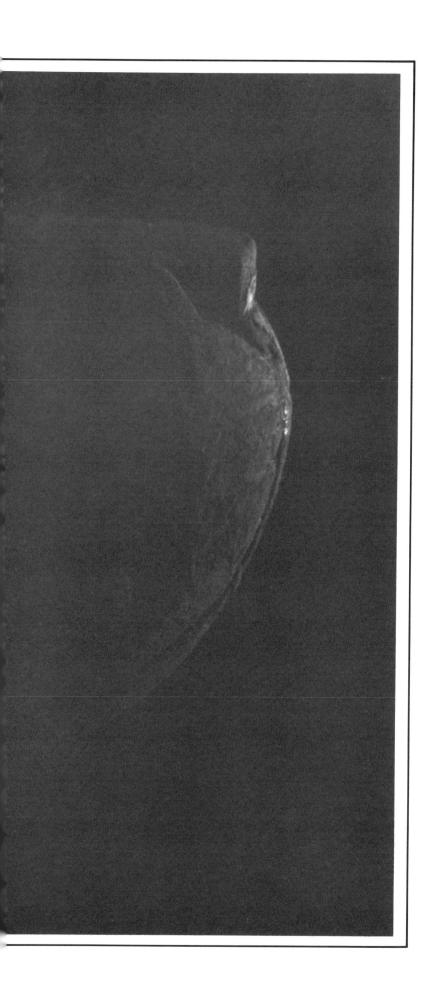

39. *BOWL*
   Cream slip on buff paste
   Hellenistic Period
   Seventh to first century B.C.
   Height 12 cm.

40a. JUG
  Green glaze on a buff paste
  Hellenistic Period
  Seventh to first century B.C.
  Height 24.7 cm.

40b. SMALL BOWL
  Gold patina on a beige paste
  Hellenistic Period
  Seventh to third century B.C.
  Height 5 cm.

41a. MINIATURE JAR
   Alabaster
   Hellenistic Period
   Height 6 cm.

41b. LARGE BOWL
   Red slip on a red paste
   Hellenistic Period
   Height 14.2 cm.

41c. JUG
   Green glaze on beige
   Hellenistic Period
   Seventh to first century B.C.
   Height 27 cm.

42. *BEADS*
   Hellenistic Period
   Seventh century B.C. to first century A.D.

43a. *JUG*
   Gold patina on a beige paste
   Hellenistic Period
   Seventh to first century B.C.
   Height 14.3 cm.

43b. *SMALL BOWL*
   Gold patina on a beige paste
   Hellenistic Period
   Height 5.5 cm.

43c. *BOWL*
   Cream slip on red paste
   Hellenistic Period
   Around 300 B.C.
   Height 11.8 cm.

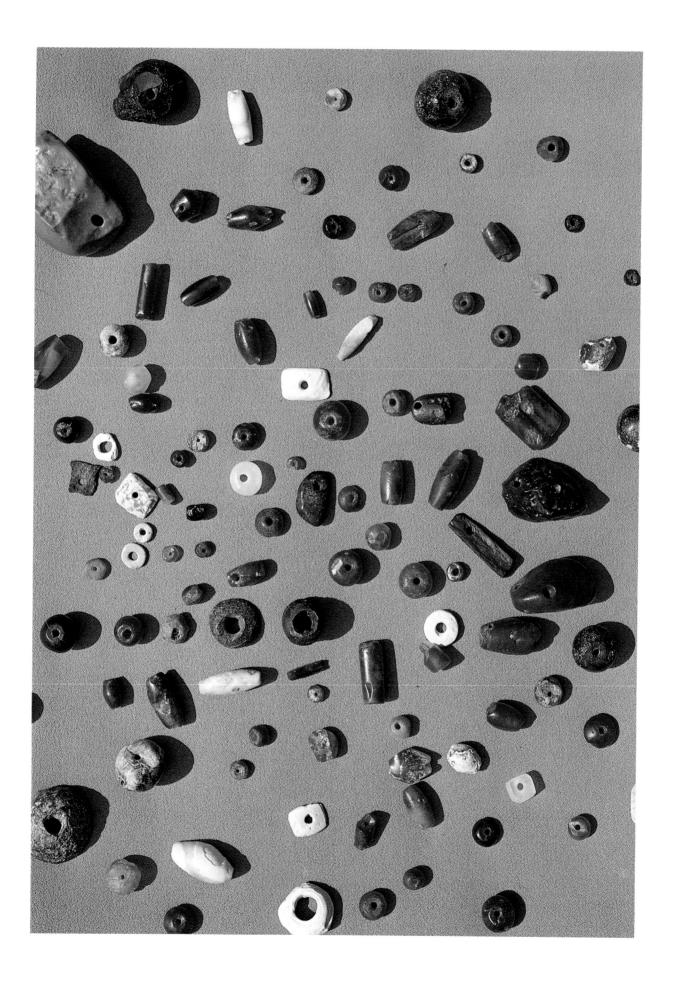

44a. EARRING
   Gold
   Hellenistic Period
   Seventh to first century B.C.
   Length 2.8 cm.

44b. FIGURINE
   Terracotta dove
   Cream slip on red paste
   Hellenistic Period
   Third century B.C. to first century A.D.
   Height without head 4.4 cm.

45a. *JAR*
   Cream paste
   Hellenistic Period
   Third century B.C. to first century A.D.
   Height 20 cm.

45b. *EARRING*
   Gold
   Sassanian Period
   Third to seventh century A.D.
   Length 2 cm.

45c. *JUG AND PLATE*
   Jug: Green glaze on cream paste
   Parthian Period
   Mid-third century B.C. to mid-third century A.D.
   Height 12.3 cm.
   Plate: Silver patina on a cream paste
   Diameter 27.8 cm.

46a. CAMEL HEADS
   Red and gray paste
   Hellenistic Period
   Third century B.C. to first century A.D.
   Tallest fragment 6 cm.

46b. JUG
   Patinated glaze on cream paste
   Hellenistic Period
   Third to first century B.C.
   Height 32 cm.

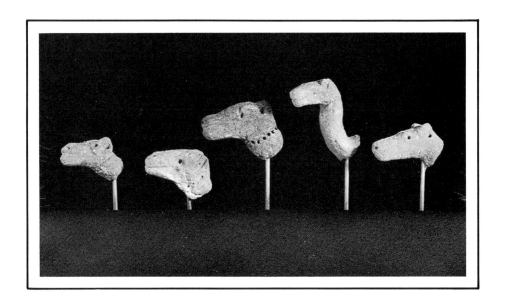

47a. STONE WITH INSCRIPTION
   Limestone
   Height of fragment 56 cm.

47b. SEAL IMPRESSION ON A SHERD
   Cream slip on red paste
   Hellenistic Period
   300 B.C. to 100 A.D.
   Length of sherd 11 cm.
   Thickness of sherd 2.5 cm.
   Diameter of impression 2.6 cm.

47c. SEAL IMPRESSION ON A
   RIM SHERD
   Cream slip on red paste
   Hellenistic Period
   300 B.C. to 100 A.D.
   Length of rim 19 cm.
   Diameter of impression 2.9 cm.

48. FIGURINES
Hellenistic Period
Third century B.C. to first century A.D.

49a. JUG
      Cream slip on buff paste
      Hellenistic Period
      300 B.C. to 100 A.D.
      Height 34 cm.

49b. BOWL
      Cream slip on a red paste
      Hellenistic Period
      Third century B.C. to first century A.D.
      Height 5.5 cm.

50. *BRONZE LIONESS*
Sassanian Period
Third to seventh century A.D.
Height 3.6 cm.

51b. CAMEL FIGURINE
Cream slip on red paste
Hellenistic Period
Third century B.C. to first century A.D.
Total length 12.5 cm.

51a. SPINDLE AND WHORLS
Bone
Spindle length 15.5 cm.
Whorls diameter ca. 2.5 cm.

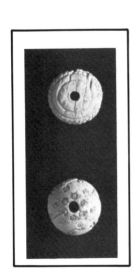

52a. *STORAGE JAR*
   Red paste
   Sassanian Period
   Third to seventh century A.D.
   Height 45.5 cm.

52b. *JAR*
   Cream slip on red paste
   Sassanian Period
   Third to seventh century A.D.
   Height 16.8 cm.

52c. *UTILITARIAN KITCHENWARE*
   Red paste
   Late Islamic
   Height 24.5 cm.

53. *JUG*
   Gray paste with copious cream-colored temper
   Height 23 cm.

54. *LARGE BOWL*
   Blue-green glaze on porous cream paste
   Late Sassanian or Early Islamic Period
   600 to 800 A.D.
   Height ca. 30 cm.

55a. *STORAGE JAR*
   Gray finish on red paste
   Third to seventh century A.D.
   Height 39.2 cm.

55b. *JUG*
   Cream paste
   Early Islamic
   Tenth century A.D.
   Height 14.3 cm.

56a. JUG
Blue-green glaze on a buff paste
Sassanian to Early Islamic
Height 27 cm.

56b. JUG
Blue-green glaze on a porous buff paste
Sassanian to Early Islamic Periods
Height 39.5 cm.

57a. *SHALLOW BOWL*
 Green glaze on molded
  apricot paste
 Islamic Period
 Ninth century
 Height 3.3 cm.

57b. *SHALLOW BOWL*
 Light gray steatite
 Islamic Period
 Height 5.9 cm.

57c. *STORAGE JAR*
 Thick blue-green glaze on porous cream paste
 Late Sassanian or Early Islamic
 Sixth to eighth century A.D.
 Height 67.5 cm.

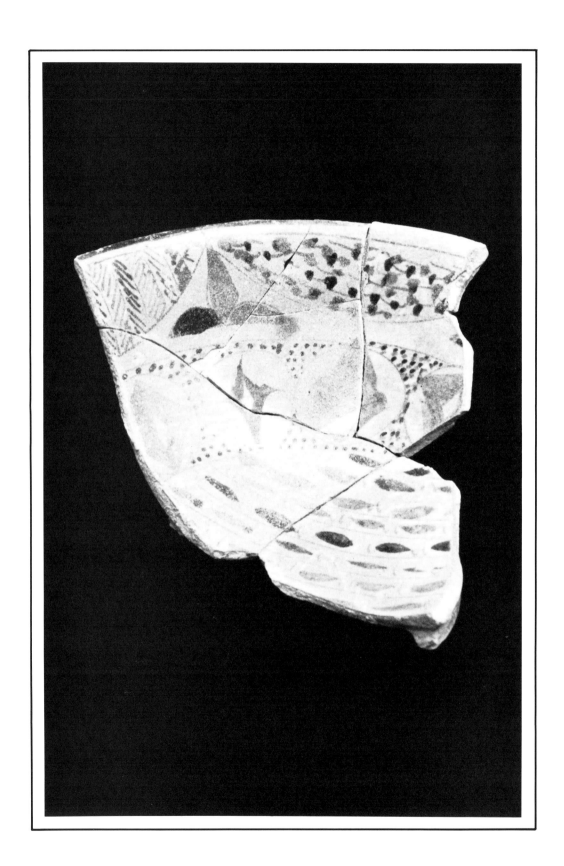
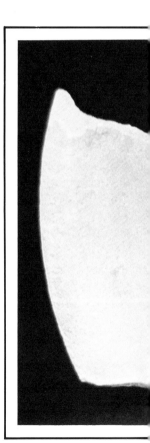

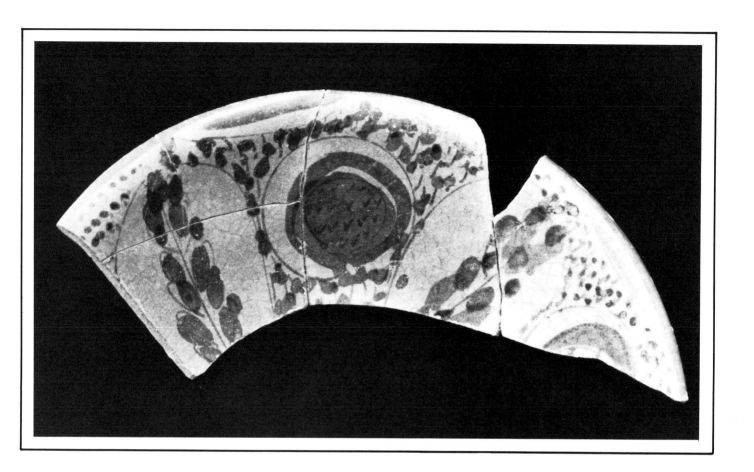

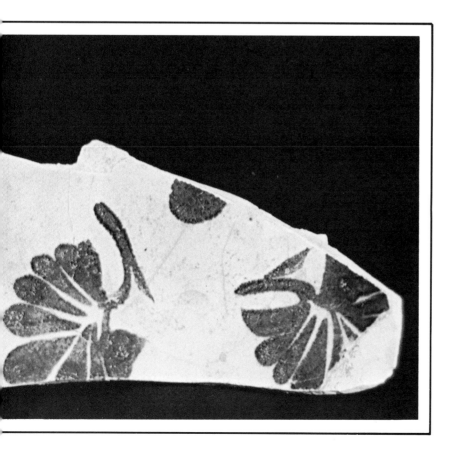

58a. BOWL FRAGMENT
   Lustre painting on cream paste
   Ninth century A.D.
   Height of bowl 10.7 cm.
   Diameter ca. 29 cm.

58b. BOWL FRAGMENT
   Lustre painting on cream paste
   Early Islamic Period
   Ninth century
   Diameter ca. 23.5 cm.

58c. BOWL FRAGMENT
   Cobalt blue design, white glaze
      on buff paste
   Islamic Period
   Ninth Century
   Height of bowl 5.5 cm.
   Diameter ca. 21.5 cm.

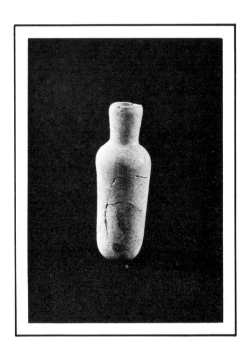

59. *SMALL BOTTLES*
   Glass
   Islamic Period

60a. *JAR*
     Cobalt and blue trim, gray glaze on porous buff paste
     Islamic Period
     Ninth century
     Height 16.5 cm.

60b. *BOWL*
     Blue-green trim, gray glaze on buff paste
     Islamic Period
     Ninth century
     Height 11 cm.

60c. *SHALLOW BOWL*
     Blue-green and black trim, gray glaze on beige paste
     Islamic Period
     Ninth century
     Height 6.8 cm.

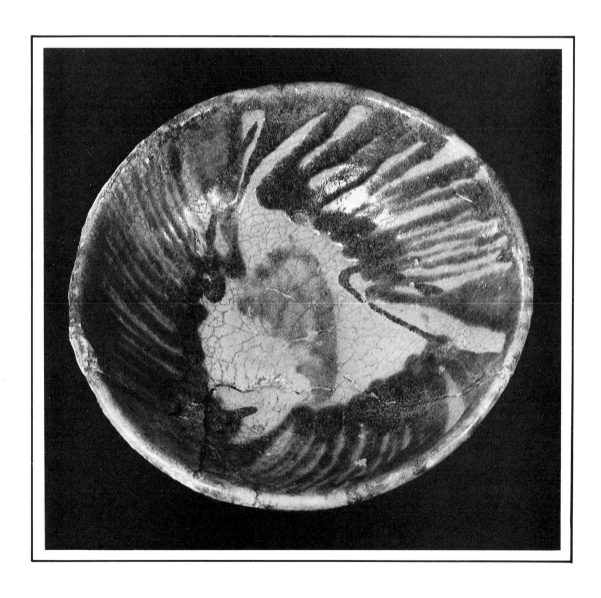

61a. BOWL
    Blue-green trim, white glaze
      on cream paste
    Islamic Period
    Ninth century
    Height 7 cm.

61b. BOWL
    Green and black trim, yellow glaze on fine apricot paste
    Islamic Period
    Ninth century
    Height 7.5 cm.

61c. BOWL
  Creamy-white glaze on cream paste
  Islamic Period
  Ninth century
  Height 8.5 cm.

61d. BOWL
  Gray glaze on a fine cream paste
  Blue-green and black decoration
  Islamic Period
  Ninth century
  Height 9 cm.

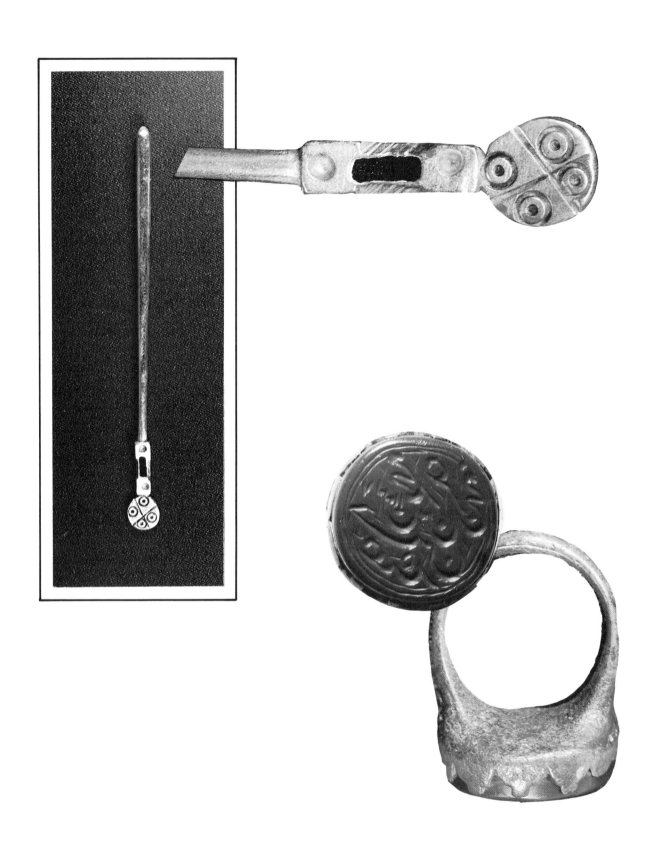

62a. EAR CLEANER
Length 11.5 cm.

62b. SEAL RING
Black stone set in silver

62c. APPLICATOR
Mother-of-pearl
Length 6.1 cm.

63a. LARGE JAR
Blue-green glaze on cream paste
Islamic Period
Twelfth century
Height 52 cm.

63b. STORAGE JAR
Buff paste
Late Islamic
Height 51 cm.

64a. *JUG*
   Cream slip on red paste
   Islamic Period
   First half of eighteenth century
   Height 17.5 cm.

64b. *LAMP*
   Blue-green glaze on cream paste
   Height 2.3 cm.

64c. *COOKPOT*
   Cream slip on red paste
   Late Islamic Period
   Seventeenth or eighteenth century
   Height 16.5 cm.

65. BRACELETS
Glass
Late Islamic Period

66a. QUERN STONES
     Islamic Period
     Diameter ca. 31 cm.

66b. PEARLING WEIGHTS, LOOM/NET WEIGHTS
Pearling weights: stone
Islamic Period
Length of largest weight 19 cm.
Weight ca. 4.1 kg.

67. *BOWL*
   Light gray steatite
   Late Islamic Period
   Height 11.2 cm.

CATALOGUE NOTES

The comment has been made that these artifacts should have been left in situ until trained archaeologists could discover and record them. In theory this is correct. However, during the 1960's when most of these items were collected, numerous other expatriates were collecting from the same areas. The possibility that this valuable material might remain on the surface until scientific tabulation could be accomplished was slim indeed.

My first significant discoveries were hand carried to the Smithsonian Institution, United States National Museum, in July, 1966. Later as I continued to search for information about the artifacts I was finding I realized how very important it was for these treasures to remain in Saudi Arabia.

My collection, donated to the Saudi Arabian Department of Antiquities in three increments, March 1968, August 1972, and January 1974, comprises a generous portion of the displays in Riyadh. The magnificent new Museum now includes a comprehensive collection ranging from paleolithic handaxes to exquisite Islamic bowls. These treasures, the property of the people of Saudi Arabia, have been preserved as a part of their cultural heritage.

The dates or periods for these artifacts which are suggested here are merely guidelines based on published material from nearby countries. These dates will, no doubt, need revision as research in this area continues.

CATALOGUE

1. HANDAXES

   Cream-colored chert

   Length of largest specimen ca. 14 cm.

   Implements such as these are usually labeled handaxes, however it is believed that they were used for a number of tasks: grubbing edible roots, cutting wood, dressing game, scraping hides, etc. These large rugged chert bifaces fit comfortably in the hand. Many of them have been found along the northern edge of the Rub' Al Khali, the great sand mountains of southeastern Arabia. Field has collected considerable information concerning flint/chert implements from various Arabian sites (Field, 1958, pp. 93, 94 and 1971, Pl. 11b-13, 29-32). Kapel reports on the flint cultures of Qatar with comparable artifacts (Kapel, 1967, Pl. 2-4). Cornwall describes a Lower Paleolithic specimen found in situ at Dawadmi "which is in the very heart of Arabia" (Cornwall, 1946, p. 39 and Pl. 8). For a more recent report on the chipped stone in the Eastern Province see Potts, et al, 1978, and Zarins, et al, 1979, for information on the Central Province.

2a, 2b. HANDAX

   Chert

   Length 11.3 cm.

   26°44+'N   49°45+'E

   A bifacially percussion-worked ovate has a sharp continuous cutting edge. Some of the cortex remains on both faces. The cross section is elliptic. Usually the chert found in the Eastern Province is a brownish black, very hard and shiny, has no crystals, and is related to flint. This specimen has two types of snail shells embedded which can be clearly distinguished under a microscope.* The handax, fashioned in the Acheulean tradition, came from a rocky hilltop overlooking an artesian well. Cornwall reports in his survey during 1940-41 that the area west of the Qatif oasis was littered with stone and flint implements (Cornwall, 1946, p. 41). Sordinas, 1973 and 1978 reports on stone implements collected from various sites in Saudi Arabia. He includes photographs of early handaxes.

   *I am indebted to Mr. Art Bowsher, through the courtesy of Mr. William Goellner, for this analysis.

3. IMPLEMENTS

   Flint/chert

   26°43'N   49°44+'E

   Representative of the recognized traditions in flint tool manufacture these implements exemplify the major types found in the Eastern Province.

   A. Flake

   Length 8.2 cm.

   Fashioned from a nodule of striped grainy chert a large thin flake has been retouched on the perimeter of both dorsal and ventral faces. It retains a sharp cutting edge near the smaller end.

B. Handax

Length 12 cm.

The symmetrical ovoid handax, comparable to the late Acheulean biface tools, has been skillfully executed from a cream-colored chert. It has a slightly crescent profile and an elliptical cross-section.

C. Blades

Longest one 7.5 cm.

Also shown here are three extremely long thin uniface blades struck from a well-prepared core and having minimal retouch on the dorsal side. Kapel classifies the Qatar cultures into A, B, C, and D (A being the oldest) and places the long blades in culture B (Kapel, 1967, Pl. 17).

4. POINTS

Flint/chert

Dozens of aceramic sites dispersed over the Eastern Province are carpeted with flint/chert implements representing countless millennia of prehistory. Some of these areas appear to have been lake beds suggesting interim changes in the environment. The points pictured here and on Plates 5 and 6 come from two of these locations, one north of Hofuf where there is a small limestone outcropping surrounded now by salt flat. Most likely it was marsh or water in ancient times. The other area appears to have been a river bed where the fresh water overflow from the Al Hasa oasis ran to the Gulf, 55 km. distant, just as it does now with the recently-installed elaborate irrigation and drainage project.

A. Tan and rose-brown chert

Length 3.9 cm.

25°38′N   49°35′E

An asymmetrical blade has marginal pressure flaking on one side. A small area at the tang end is retouched on the reverse. The cross-section is trapezoidal.

B. Striped honey-colored chert

Length 5.8 cm.

25°38′N   49°35′E

Triangular in cross-section this elongated blade has marginal pressure flaking on both surfaces. A large uneven scar suggests that it was probably rejected during manufacture.

C. Mottled chert

Length 6.5 cm.

25°49+′N   50°03+′E

An elongated uniface blade trapezoidal in cross-section has an S-twist from tang to point. There is minimal pressure flaking on the dorsal surface.

D. Light to medium brown chert

Length 4.4 cm.

25°38′N   49°35′E

An elongated asymmetrical blade has a fine pressure-flaked margin along the point on the dorsal side. The ventral is pressure flaked and narrowed at the tang for hafting.

E. Good quality medium brown chert

Length 3.4 cm.

25°38′N   49°35′E

A lanceolate blade, triangular in cross-section, has a finely worked point. The ventral has pressure retouching at the point.

5. POINTS
   A. Light brown flint
      Length 3.8 cm.
      25°38′N   49°35′E
An elongated blade is triangular in cross-section, crescent shaped in longitudinal profile. The tang has been formed by the removal of several flakes on each edge of the dorsal side and narrowed on the tip of the ventral. Marginal pressure flaking is confined to both edges of the dorsal.
   B. Light brown chert
      Length 3.5 cm.
      25°38′N   49°35′E
An extremely sharp tanged blade, triangular in cross-section, is pressure worked on the dorsal side but unretouched on the ventral except for the narrowing of the tang by the removal of several tiny flakes.
   C. Light brown flint
      Length 4.3 cm.
      25°38′N   49°35′E
A bifacially pressure-flaked point with a symmetrical isosceles tip is elliptical in cross-section. The small barbs are formed by the careful removal of a large flake on each side.
   D. Medium brown flint
      Length 3.6 cm.
      25°49+′N   50°03+′E
An asymmetrical elongated blade has flakes removed on the dorsal side to produce a tang. The ventral has minimal pressure flaking to narrow the tang. Aeolian action has left a beautiful polish on both faces.
   E. Light orange flint
      Length 2.5 cm.
      25°49+′N   50°03+′E
A small symmetrically bifacially worked arrowhead is carefully pressure flaked to produce an even edge. One barb is slightly larger than the other. Wind action has left a glossy appearance on both faces.

6. POINTS
   Flint/chert
   A. Light brown flint
      Length 3.8 cm.
      25°49+′N   50°03+′E
A bifacially-worked point is concavo-convex in profile. The thickness is only 0.4 cm. Flake scars are shallow and irregular. There is considerable evidence of aeolin action.
   B. Brown streaked chert of poor quality
      Length 5.4 cm.
      25°38′N   49°35′E
A bifacially-worked thin symmetrical foliate point is rather poorly flaked probably due to the inferior quality of the chert. Marginal retouch is minimal. The cross-section is elliptic.

7. BEAKER

Black mat paint on yellow-green paste
'Ubaid 3 Period
End of the sixth millennium B.C.
Height 10.1 cm.
27°09'N   49°19+'E

The exterior of the eggshell thin pottery has been water smoothed. A five-petal design decorates the rounded bottom. The upper design depicts small fish swimming into angular fish traps.* For a cup from the tombs at Eridu with a similiar design see Mallowan, 1965, Illus. 12.

A C-14 determination taken from shells just below the beaker give a date of 6157 B.P. ± 238 years. When allowances are made for the known variation in C-14 dates for the fifth millennium, the true date may be estimated at 5057 B.C. ± 288 years. For an account of the discovery of 'Ubaid pottery in Arabia see Burkholder, 1971, pp. 264-269.

*Pat Johnston of Ras Tanura first called attention to this interpretation.

8. BEAKER

(See Pl. 7)
This exquisite drawing of the beaker pictured in Pl. 7 was executed by Pat Johnston.

9a. AWL

Light orange flint
'Ubaid Period
ca. 5000 B.C.
26°54+'N   49°44+'E

Miniature awls similar to this one have been found at several Arabian 'Ubaid sites. The smallest one measures no more than 0.5 cm. in length. This one is from Site 1 from which we have a C-14 determination from shells taken 15 cm. below the surface. The date of 6135 B.P. ± 120 years, when converted for the known variation is radiocarbon readings for the fifth millennium B.C., suggests 5000 B.C. as a terminal date for this site. The purpose for fashioning such tiny implements is of course controversial, but the possibility of their being used to drill holes in pearls cannot be ignored.

9b. BOWL

Straw-tempered buff paste
'Ubaid Period
Fifth millennium B.C.
Height 16.3 cm.
27°25'N   49°13'E

Found at Arabian 'Ubaid Site 29, this flat-bottomed bowl has slightly flared sides that narrow in thickness as they rise. The badly-weathered buff paste contains small amounts of straw tempering. Straw-tempered sherds have been recorded from nine Arabian 'Ubaid sites. Many have copious tempering and show signs of burning on lower sections. Some have small knob handles attached. For a photograph of straw-tempered sherds from Arabian Site 11 see Burkholder, 1971, pp. 268, 269.

9c. JUG

Black paint, cream slip on a red paste
'Ubaid Period
Early fifth millennium B.C.
Height 26 cm.

A black mat paint covers the straight neck, the slightly flared spout, and ends in a somewhat oblique line on the shoulder below which appear a row of dots. Another single painted band encircles the handmade vessel close to the round bottom. Mallowan describes rings such as these being popular at Gawra (Mallowan, 1967, p. 70). The closest published parallels are from Ur where a number of almost straight necks appear on round bottoms. However, none have the same flared spout nor duplicate the decoration (Woolley, 1956, fig. 41, 52, 56, 58, 60, 70). This jug, from a private collection, is reported to have been found at the eastern extremity of the Al Hasa Oasis.

10. VASE

Light gray steatite
Proto-Dynastic Period
End of the fourth millennium B.C.
Height 11.5 cm.
26°33+'N   50°04+'E

On this unique flat-bottomed vase with an outcurving rim two zebu follow each other under a canopy of vegetation. From the tops of the zebus' heads water flows backward and ends in a graceful swirl with a mother-of-pearl inlay. Additional inlays decorate the large loose skin of the neck, dewlap, and also the nautilis shells (?) between the animals' legs. Prominent male features are shown on the sturdy bodies. The animals stand on the bottom of the vase with the spaces between them filled by oblique parallel lines. Very similar is the animal on the Khafaje vase. See Strommenger for an excellent photograph (Strommenger, 1964, Pl. 38). This vessel is in a private collection.

11. VASE

(See Pl. 10)

Pat Johnston of Ras Tanura has rendered this drawing of the vase shown in Pl. 10.

12. SPOUTED JUG

Traces of black paint on a gray paste
which includes a light colored temper
Protoliterate Period
Late fourth to early third millennium B.C.
Height 22.2 cm.
Purchased in Qatif

The wheel-thrown spouted jug appears to have been constructed in two sections which were fitted together before firing.* The upper section is finished rather well while the lower body is crudely fashioned. Perkins associates this technique with the Warka and Protoliterate periods at Jamdat Nasr (Perkins, 1949, p. 106). Evidence of black paint, though considerably worn, still remains on the interior, exterior, and also on the flat bottom.

*Dr. During-Caspers, Leiden, noted this technique when she examined the vessel.

13. BOWL

Light gray steatite
Proto-Dynastic Period
End of the fourth millennium B.C.
Height 7 cm.
26°33+'N   50°04+'E

A fragment of a shallow bowl with vertical sides has a kneeling figure between two snakes. The outstretched palms touch but do not grasp the elliptically-pitted bodies. Pits such as these on similar pieces sometimes contain a colored paste or mother-of-pearl inlay. The long hair, shown with sections of incised lines placed in alternating directions, ends in a loose fall below the waist. Strommenger pictures the Khafaje bowl which has a somewhat similar figure (Strommenger, 1964, Pl. 38). Zarins, 1978, reports on the steatite in the Riyadh museum.

14. CUPS

Left: cream slip on beige paste
Center: cream slip on red paste
Right: cream slip on beige paste
Height ca. 14 cm.
26°33+'N   50°04+'E

These wheel-thrown cups have slipped exteriors with shaved lower sections. The shape is similar to Jamdat Nasr cups from Ur (Woolley, 1956, Pl. 60, JN 107). Perkins reports another example from Warka (Perkins, 1949, fig. 12 No. 8).

15a. BOWL

Dark gray serpentine
Early Dynastic Period
First half of the third millennium B.C.
Height 5.8 cm.
26°33+'N   50°04+'E

This little bowl was mended in antiquity with tiny holes, twelve of which remain, four drilled from the exterior and eight from the interior. The design of the bowl is remarkable in that, if tipped, it immediately rights itself. The shape is similar to one from Tepe Yahya (Lamberg-Karlovsky, 1970, Pl. 24). Also see Woolley, 1934, Pl. 177. Plate 18b. depicts another bowl of this shape. I am indebted to Dr. William Greenwood, United States Geological Survey, Jiddah, for his identification of the stone as serpentine.

15b. ANIMAL FIGURINE

Red paste
End of the fourth millennium B.C.
Height 3 cm.
25°34 'N   49°38+'E

The small badly weathered figurine quite possibly represents a pig. Its origin, close to the old lakebed at Hofuf, reinforces this hypothesis. There is a single deep hole where the mouth normally would be located.

15c. BEAKER

Cream slip on red paste
Pre-Barbar Period
Early third millennium B.C.
Height 7.5 cm.
25°34+'N   49°37+'E

A very poor example of handmade pottery, this flat-bottomed beaker has slip on both exterior and interior surfaces. The site where it was found has been identified as pre-Barbar.

15d. BOWL

Light gray steatite
Height 7.1 cm.
26°33+'N   50°04+'E

Light streaks create an interesting pattern in this smoothly-finished bowl. Fine circular scratches show on the interior. The rim is flattened on top. A single deep groove separates the foot from the body.

16a. MINIATURE VASE

Travertine marble
Early third millennium B.C.
Height 4.8 cm.
26°33+'N   50°04+'E

Miniature in size but graceful in design, a little vase depicts the same contour as the larger vases recovered from Ur, Mari, and more recently the Barbar Temple on Bahrain (Mortensen, 1970, p. 396). See also Woolley, 1956, Pl. 34 and Woolley, 1934, Pl. 176).

16b. BOWL

Translucent marble with copper-colored veins
Proto-Dynastic Period
End of the fourth millennium B.C.
Diameter 9.7 cm.
26°33+'N   50°04+'E

Mended in antiquity, seven of the tiny drilled holes remain. Three are plugged with a deposit which appears to be a light colored fiberous residue. The bottom is slightly convex. Similar bowls have been found at Ur, Telloch, Jamdat Nasr, and Khafaje (Perkins, 1949, pp. 136-137 and fig. 18, No.1). Dr. William Greenwood, after examining this vessel, classified the material as translucent marble.

16c. BOWL

Translucent marble with copper-colored veins
Proto-Dynastic Period
End of the fourth millennium B.C.
Diameter 10.9 cm.
26°33+'N   50°04+'E

The heavy convex bottom is 2.0 cm. thick. See Woolley for bowls of similar shape with heavy bottoms (Woolley, 1956, Pl. 65, No. 16).

17a. JAR

Buff paste
Jamdat Nasr Period
End of fourth to early third millennium B.C.
Height 20.5 cm.
26°33+'N   50°04+'E

Typical of the Jamdat Nasr vessels from Ur, this wheel-thrown jar has a sharp carination high on the shoulder and a drooping beaded rim. The small bottom is slightly convex (Woolley, 1956, Pl. 57 JN44). Many Jamdat Nasr jugs have spouts attached at the shoulder. This one is broken in such a manner that we cannot tell whether or not it was spouted. Recent finds of Jamdat Nasr ware on Bahrain, in Abu Dhabi and in Oman make the appearance of this type less spectacular here.

17b. JAR

Black paint, cream slip on red paste
Umm an Nar Period
Second quarter of the third millennium B.C.
Height 19.5 cm.
26°34+'N   50°03+'E

Many fine examples of Umm an Nar pottery in addition to this very weathred flat-bottomed jar come from Tarut. In 1959 the Danish expedition first excavated the thin painted ware on a small island off the coast of Abu Dhabi (Bibby, 1969, pp. 273-281). Since then it has been found on Bahrain and at the Oasis of Al-Ain. Frifelt has suggested a date of 2700 B.C. as the beginning of this culture (Frifelt, 1971, p. 298).

18a. BOWL

Translucent marble
Jamdat Nasr Period
End of fourth to early third millennium B.C.
Height 11.9 cm.
26°33+'N   50°04+'E

This heavy vessel has a thick bottom (1.9 cm.) and sides that narrow gradually as they rise and incurve slightly just below the plain inverted "V" rim. See Woolley, 1956, Pl. 65 JN4 which has an identical shape except that it is round-bottomed while the Arabian example has a flat bottom 6 cm. in diameter.

18b. BOWL

Dark gray serpentine
Early Dynastic Period
First half of the third millennium B.C.
Height 5 cm.
26°33+'N   50°04+'E

The thin flaring sides of this small bowl are fashioned in a graceful "S" curve. A small base protrudes 2 mm. Like the bowl in Pl. 15a, this vessel is designed in such a manner that, if tipped, it rights itself.

18c. BOWL

Banded marble
Early Dynastic Period
First half of the third millennium B.C.
Height 3.5 cm.
26°33+'N   50°04+'E

A small bowl of white marble streaked with black has the rim and carination of Royal Cemetery stone vessels (Woolley, 1956, Pl. 69 RC109).

19a. BOWL

Light gray steatite
First half of the third millennium B.C.
Height 4.7 cm.
26°33+'N   50°04+'E

A round-bottomed shallow bowl with a flat rim is decorated with a row of dotted circles placed between incised lines. The dotted circle is a design that found popularity at Umm an Nar early in the third millennium B.C. and continued to be used by different cultures into Islamic times. See Frifelt, 1970, fig. 14 and p. 379. Delougaz reports a number of vessels from the Larsa period with this design (Delougaz, 1952, Pl. 123).

19b. BOWL

Light gray steatite
Jamdat Nasr Period
End of fourth to early third millennium B.C.
Height 7.9 cm.
26°33+'N   50°04+'E

A very chalky porous steatite with a smooth finish is the material from which this vessel was fashioned. The exterior bottom is badly weathered however a tiny area indicates there was originally a small foot. A similar bowl of limestone is pictured by Woolley, 1956, Pl. 32.

19c. VASE

Light gray steatite
Jamdat Nasr Period
End of fourth to early third millennium B.C.
Height 12 cm.
26°33+'N   50°04+'E

Typical of many of the deep steatite vessels, the inner surface seems quite crude when compared with the smooth exterior. The hyperbolic shape in conjunction with the flat bottom resembles that of a Jamdat Nasr vase excavated at Ur (Woolley, 1956, Pl. 34 U.19513).

20a. MINIATURE BOWLS

Coarse cream paste
Early second millennium B.C.
Diameter ca. 9 cm.
26°33+'N 50°04+'E

These small bowls have been recovered by the gardeners on Tarut in considerable quantities. Often ten or more were found together in the earth. Since the crumbly cream paste fractures easily and the bowls appear so poorly made, one is lead to believe they could not withstand normal usage. Consequently their manufacture must have been designed with minimal usage in mind such as funerary or foundation deposits. The inturning rim makes their use as a drinking vessel impossible. See Delougaz, 1952, Pl. 120c and 148 for similar shapes.

20b. BOWL

Light gray steatite
Jamdat Nasr Period
End of fourth to early third millennium B.C.
Height 15 cm.
26°33+'N 50°04+'E

A large symmetrical bowl has its maximum diameter close to the rounded bottom. The sides taper gradually in thickness from 1.3 cm. and end in a smooth envelope-thin rim 18.2 cm. in diameter. It would seem that this rather plain shape might be easy to manufacture and, consequently, would be quite popular, but instead, among the dozens of published stone bowl types only one parallel has been found (Woolley, 1956, Pl. 65 JN4).

21a. BEAKER

Argillaceous limestone with coral inclusions*
Early third millennium B.C.
Height 8.8 cm.
26°33+'N 50°04+'E

This small beaker has been carved from a very attractive black stone which has white streaks running through it. The bottom is flat. *Mr. Art Bowsher identified the stone for us through the courtesy of Mr. William Goellner. Mr. Bowsher comments that the coral is Upper Paleozoic era, probably Permian. Lamberg-Karlovsky found similar worked fragments at Tepe Yahya (personal communication).

21b. MACEHEAD

Marble
Early Dynasitc Period
First half of the third millennium B.C.
Diameter 6 cm.
26°33+'N 50°04+'E

The drilled opening 1.5 cm. in diameter and 3.0 cm. in depth tapers toward the bottom. That maceheads of stone were used as early as the 'Ubaid period is recorded by Woolley, 1956, p. 21. It is doubtful that this macehead would predate the other marble itmes from Tarut.

22a. MIRROR

Copper/bronze
Length 11.5 cm.
26°33+′N 50°04+′E

Small mirrors have been found at numerous locations. Khan reports examples from Kulli, Mohenjodaro, Hissar and Susa (Khan, 1964, Pl. XXI). From the Persian copper coffins at Ur comes another mirror made of speculum bronze (Woolley, 1962, Pl. 24).

22b. COPPER/BRONZE POINTS

Largest one 30 cm.
26°33+′N 50°04+′E

These copper/bronze points were recovered separately from the gardens of Tarut. One has a hollow shaft. Woolley excavated a copper spear point, similar to the smallest one, and a hollow-shafted harpoon at Ur (Woolley, 1956, Pl. 30). Also see Lamberg-Karlovsky, 1970, Pl. 20 for an illustration of a copper/bronze dagger from Tepe Yahya. From the Island of Failaka another collection is reported by the Kuwait Government Press, 1964, fig. 48.

22c. BOWL

Light gray steatite
First half of the third millennium B.C.
Height 10 cm.
26°33+′N 50°04+′E

On this large steatite bowl a flat foot protrudes below the graceful flaring sides. A ring-based bowl of this shape was excavated from Level IVB at Tepe Yahya and subsequently dated 3000 to 2500 B.C. (Lamberg-Karlovsky, 1970, Pl. 24 and fig.23).

23. BOWL FRAGMENT

Iron-stained muscovite schist
Early Dynastic Period
First half of the third millennium B.C.
Height 15.4 cm.
26°33+′N 50°04+′E

An iron-stained muscovite schist was used to fashion this bowl. The sparkling red-orange stone resembles sunstone commonly sold by dealers in Jiddah, however, the sample isn't quite as hard. The moscovite schist comes from the shield rather than from the sedimentary formation and occurs in a wide arc behind Jizan.* The bowl has the entwined elliptically-pitted snake which was popular on carved steatite bowls found on Tarut (Burkholder, 1971, Pl. VII and p. 321).

*Dr. William Greenwood has furnished this analysis for us through the good office of R.L. Maby.

24a. BEAD

Shell
Early third millennium B.C.
Maximum diameter ca. 2.5 cm.
25°48+'N   49°41+'E

A slightly concave shell fragment has an off-center hole drilled from the outside. Worn smooth, it appears buff colored now but is probably mother-of-pearl that has deteriorated with age. It was found with the tubular beads pictured here, from the Abqaiq salt mine tumuli area.

24b. BEADS

Ceramic, red paste
Early third millennium B.C.
Length ca. 3.5 cm.
25°48+'N   49°41+'E

From the area of the Abqaiq salt mine tumuli come these cylindrical beads which appear to have been fashioned around a thin rod which was pulled out before firing. The openings measure about .25 cm. in diameter. Some of the beads are highly burnished. One bead of the same shape, but not pictured here, is carved from a thick section of mother-of-pearl shell.

24c. JUG

Red paste
Early third millennium B.C.
Height 16.5 cm.
25°48+'N   49°42+'E

A straight neck joins the rounded body in a gentle curve. The entire rim is missing. Although this jug is restored from many fragments, a central hole ca. 1.5 cm. in diameter in the flat bottom seems deliberate. This vessel is from the area of the Abqaiq salt mine where over a thousand rock tumuli are located on a high plateau. On one of these, rock collectors had removed the entire tumulus above ground level leaving the outline of a small stone chamber exposed in a ring of limestone rock still partially imbedded in the earth. Some of the fragments of this jug were under the remaining stones of the tumulus. Burney, in reporting on the late Chalcolithic period at Yanik Tepe, describes a similiar-shaped jug (Burney, 1962, Pl. XLIII No. 4).

25. MINIATURE VESSEL

Polished light gray steatite
First half of the third millennium B.C.
Height 4.2 cm.
26°33+'N   50°04+'E

The circular opening is 5 mm. in diameter and 2.9 cm. deep. The dotted-circle design is repeated on all four sides. Tiny tool marks in the form of oblique parallel lines are visible on the finished vertical edges. This design appears as early as Tepe Yahya, Level IVB (the eye of a dog) and was very popular on Umm an Nar and Hili steatite vessels. It continues to appear frequently in the Larsa period and reoccurs into Islamic times. See Lamberg-Karlovsky, 1970, Pl. 25 and also Frifelt, 1970, p. 379 and fig. 14.

194

26. GLOBULAR BOWL

Water-smoothed exterior on reddish-buff paste
Early third millennium B.C.
Maximum diameter 15.3 cm.
25°34+'N   49°37+'E

This handmade, hole-mouthed bowl comes from a site near Hofuf that has been identified as pre-Barbar. The rim everts slightly and somewhat unevenly. From all indications this vessel had a round bottom.

27a. BOWL FRAGMENT

Light gray steatite
Early third millennium B.C.
Height ca. 13.5 cm.
Diameter ca. 25 cm.
26°33+'N   50°04'E

A guilloche ornamentation placed between two horizontal bands decorates the exterior of this bowl fragment. The bowl's sides are vertical. The areas enclosed in the bands and the guilloche have been left rough to receive an inlay while the remaining surfaces between the design and the band are quite smooth. During Jamdat Nasr and Early Dynastic periods inlays of colored stone, shell and paste were quite popular. Excellent photographs of two early vessels decorated in this manner are shown in Strommenger, 1964, Pl. VI.

27b. SMALL JAR

Polished light gray steatite
Early Dynastic Period II or III
Middle of the third millennium B.C.
Height 7.7 cm.
26°33+'N   50°04+'E

This carefully-designed jar has been decorated in a guilloche which has six, or in a few instances seven, parallel lines incised in the ornamentation. The pattern is repeated fourteen times in each of two bands which are divided by a horizontal ridge repeated once at the top and twice at the flat base. The upper and lower guilloche are strategically placed so that the oblique lines of one row complement those in the other, quite an accomplishment considering that the jar is narrower at the top of the design. The thick walls, ca. 1.0 cm., although highly polished on the exterior, are crudely finished on the interior possibly because of the narrow opening. Durrani includes four vessels from Mari with this design along with various interpretations for it (Durrani, 1964, Pl. I, IV, VI, VII, pp. 72-73, 78, 84 and 86). DuRy has an excellent photograph of a somewhat similar shaped vase from Susa now in the Louvre (DuRy, 1969, p. 76).

28a. BOWL

Light gray steatite
First half of third millennium B.C.
Height 9 cm.
26°33+'N   50°04+'E

A portion of the rim has been reconstructed with plaster. The squarish bottom gradually changes shape to become a circular-rimmed vessel. The lower section of the interior is rounded.

28b. JAR WITH BOWL

Jar: burnished red paste
Bowl: buff paste
Early Dynastic Period
First half of the third millennium B.C.
Diameter of jar rim 12 cm.
26°33+'N   50°04+'E

A small bowl closes the neck of this large storage jar which has the distinctive thickened elongated rim associated with the Early Dynastic period. The fine red paste is flaking off due to the harsh effects of the highly saline local soil. Burnished exteriors appear on a number of similar-shaped rims here. This style has been found from Ur to Abu Dhabi. See Woolley, 1934, Pl. 254 No. 61. Frifelt has more recent information from excavations in Abu Dhabi (Frifelt, 1970, p. 376 and fig. 6).

28c. MINIATURE SPOUTED VESSEL

Cream slip on red paste
Larsa Period
Early second millennium B.C.
Height 8.7 cm.
26°33+'N   50°04+'E

Another spouted miniature recovered here was reported to have had a small bowl inverted over the top. This bowl was similar to the ones in Pl. 20a. Delougaz reports a small spouted vessel from the Larsa period (Delougaz, 1952, Pl. 119, p. 117). Burney excavated another at Yanik Tepe in northwest Iran (Burney, 1961, Pl. LXX). A bronze vessel, larger but of a similar shape, is described by Frankfort. It was recovered in the excavation of the Sin Temple at Khafaje (Frankfort, 1935, p. 42).

29.a VASE

Travertine marble
Early Dynastic Period
Height 29 cm.
26°33+'N   50°04+'E

Several of these tall vases with graceful incurving sides have been excavated from pre-Dynastic graves at Ur (Woolley, 1934, Pl. 241 No. 6). More recently a tall vase which appears to have parallel sides was recovered from the temple of Barbar (Mortensen, 1970, pp. 396-397 and fig. 7). Dr. William Greenwood, United States Geological Survey, Jiddah, classifies this stone as travertine marble and states that it is not known in precambian of Saudi Arabia.

196

29b. SPOUTED JUG FRAGMENT

Cream slip on buff paste
Early Dynastic Period
First half of the third millennium B.C.
Diameter of rim ca. 13 cm.
26°22′N   50°12+′E

The rim, flat on top, protrudes in a square ledge beyond the straight short neck. The globular body has a short spout high on the shoulder. Rims of this type are depicted by Woolley and assigned to the Early Dynastic period (Woolley, 1934, Pl. 257). However spouted globular bodies were popular in the preceeding Jamdat Nasr period (Woolley, 1956, Pl. 63).

29c. INCENSE BURNER

Light gray steatite
Early first millennium B.C.
Height 6.5 cm.
26°54+′N   49°32′E

The dotted-circle design is repeated six times in a vertical row between incised lines on each leg. The design appears again in a horizontal band of four sections: six circles in the first, five in the second, and an indeterminate number in the third. The handle is attached to the fourth section. The short legs, one of which is restored with plaster, are wedge-shaped. This vessel appears to be a prototype of the square, four-legged incense burners found at Thaj. Cleveland described a circular tripod offering saucer fashioned from alabaster which has wedge-shaped legs but no handle (Cleveland, Pl. 90 and p. 117).

30. JAR

Black mat paint on yellow-green paste
Last half of the third millennium B.C.
Height 16 cm.
26°33+′N   50°04+′E

This delicate thin-walled jar thrown on a fast wheel has a small flared foot at the otherwise flat bottom. The rim, flattened on top, repeats the shape of the foot. Closest parallels for this artistically-painted vessel are found in the Indus Valley. The Amri culture has the thin-walled vessels of similar shape, whereas the Harappan culture makes use of the pipal leaf to fill the surfaces of a pot. The graceful painted foliage certainly belongs to this style of decoration. See Khan, 1964, fig. 9, Pl. XLIV No. 1, p. 58.

31. JAR

(See Plate 30)

Pat Johnston has reproduced here the flowered motif decorating the jar shown in Pl. 30.

32a. SEAL

Light gray steatite
Barbar Period
Late third millennium B.C.
Diameter 2.1 cm.
26°33+'N 50°04+'E

Carved from steatite, this seal with its indeterminate design has an undecorated, pierced, convex back. For examples of other Gulf seals see Porada, 1971, p. 332, and Pl. IX, X.

32b. STORAGE VESSEL FRAGMENTS

Cleam slip on red paste
Barbar Period
Late third millennium B.C.
Left: diameter of rim 9.2 cm.
Right: diameter of rim ca. 11.5 cm.
26°33+'N 50°04+'E

The red paste of these large storage vessels shows yellow specks throughout. A sample of clay taken from the cliffs on Jebel Bohara displayed the same peculiar yellow specks when fired. These vessels with their perforated necks quite likely were the type used for beverages. Daniel tells us that the Sumerians placed a jar of beer on the floor between them and drank through long metal tubes (Daniel, 1968, p. 74). A seal found on Bahrain depicts this scene (Bibby, 1969, p. 382). Porada gives us the background information for this interpretation and relates that this practice of drinking through tubes had been very popular in Early Dynastic and continued into the Akkad period (Porada, 1971, p. 335).

32c. JUG

Red paste speckled with yellow
Barbar Period
Late third millennium B.C.
Height 17 cm.
26°34+'N 50°03+'E

The pinched ridges, typical of the period, start about 5 cm. below the beveled rim and continue approximately 1 cm. apart to the bottom of the vessel which is slightly concave and 5.0 cm. in diameter. The ridges wind around the vessel in a continuous spiral. For other Barbar jugs see Bibby, 1969, Pl. XV, XVI.

33. JUG

Red paint, cream slip on buff paste
Akkadian Period
Third quarter of third millennium B.C.
Height 17 cm.
26°33+'N   50°04+'E

Typical of those found in Akkadian graves, this vessel has a long neck on a squat conical body. Traces of red paint are evident on the underside of the rim, neck, and over 1 cm. on the shoulder. Below this only a cream slip remains in spots on the badly eroded surface. For reference check Porada, 1965, fig. V No. 14 and Delougaz, 1952, Pl. 160.

34a. LIMESTONE SHEEP

Height 6.5 cm.
26°33+'N   50°04+'E

To furnish a delightful toy for a child, a cult figurine to increase the fertility of the flock, or a symbolic sacrifice for an altar may explain the sculptor's intention for this small stylized sheep. The white limestone image has no special features such as eyes or mouth.

34b. LION SCULPTURE

Limestone
Height 16.8 cm.
26°33+'N   50°04+'E

Although badly weathered, this sculpture retains discernible features on one side. The eyes are circular in shape and consist of two raised circles, the inner one being quite prominent. Behind them are two knobbed ears. The mouth is represented by a deep recess measuring 2 x 5 cm. on each profile. It may be that these recesses were designed for an inlay.

35a. JUG

Burnished red paste
Hellenistic Period
Seventh to third century B.C.
Height 21 cm.
26°33+'N   50°04+'E

A cordon placed 3.5 cm. above the flat base, a tiny ridge where the neck joins the body, and a row of fine combing on the shoulder create an attractive jug.

35b. BOWL

Red wash on olive green paste
Hellenistic Period
Seventh to third centuries B.C.
Height 6.7 cm.
25°49'N   50°02+'E

A poorly executed warped bowl with traces of red wash on the exterior. The bottom is flat. This bowl was found at the area local people refer to as "Gerrha." See Plates 35c, 38a, and 42.

35c. COPPER/BRONZE POINTS

Hellenistic Period
Seventh century B.C. to first century A.D.
Longest specimen 6 cm.
25°53+'N   50°00+'E

Many bronze points have been found at the location termed "Gerrha" by local amateur archaeologists. For an aerial photograph of this site showing the vast irrigation network see Linton, 1961, pp. 24-26. The Danish expedition examined this area in 1968 in connection with their reconnaissance of the Eastern Province (Bibby, 1969, pp. 317, 328, 372-373). Frifelt reports on bronze points recovered in Oman (Frifelt, 1970, p. 365).

36a. JUG

Cream slip on red paste
Hellenistic Period
Seventh century B.C.
Height 20.5 cm.
Purchased in Qatif

A slightly concave base finishes the bottom of this jug. A duplicate jug, slightly larger in diameter, was excavated by the Danish expedition on Bahrain in the City IV Palace (Bibby, 1964, p. 86, fig. 1).

36b. MINIATURE JUG

Red wash on buff paste
Selucid Period
Third to first century B.C.
Height 4.7 cm.
Purchased in Qatif

A bright red wash covers the exterior of this tiny jug. The shoulder is decorated by a slight groove placed 1.6 cm. below the rim. Another miniature was excavated from Charsada I, layer 22 (Wheeler, 1962, fig. 25).

36c. BOWL

Gray finish on a red paste
Hellenistic Period
Height 4.6 cm.
26°34+'N   50°03+'E

The lightly incised horizontal lines are the only decoration on this water-smoothed bowl which has been fired in a reducing kiln to obtain a gray finish. A small flat bottom measures 3.5 cm. in diameter.

37. SCULPTURE

Limestone
Height 50 cm.
26°34+'N   50°03+'E

A featureless (?) limestone sculpture with a rounded head on a rectangular body is more nearly like the sculptures in alabaster from South Arabia than the mother-goddess figurines of the Mesopotamian area. Doe furnishes an excellent account of the South Arabian figures (Doe, 1971, Pl. VI). Also see DuRy for a sandstone idol ca. 2000 B.C. in the National Museum, Aleppo, and a funerary statue in limestone from Yemen (DuRy, 1969, pp. 189, 254).

38a. JUG

Greenish-gray paste
Hellenistic Period
Seventh to third century B.C.
Height 21 cm.
25°49+'N   50°03+'E

A Hellenistic jug, thrown on a wheel, slightly asymmetrical, has three deep lines as its sole decoration. The sides splay slightly where they meet the flat bottom.

38b. MINIATURE BOWL

Bright red slip on red paste
Third century B.C. to seventh century A.D.
Height 5.5 cm.
26°34+'N   50°03+'E

A hole, 0.5 cm. in diameter, has been drilled through the center of the round bottom. A flat rim finishes the top. The use of orange to red slip is not common here. Whitehouse and Williamson explain its origin and occurrence at Siraf (Whitehouse and Williamson, 1973, p. 38).

38c. BOWL

Beige paste with a brownish patina
Hellenistic Period
Third century B.C.
Height 4.8 cm.
26°33+'N   50°04+'E

A delicate, thin, wheel-thrown bowl has minute traces of green in the patina to indicate the original color. A concave foot finishes the bottom. A published parallel from the Greek fortress on Failaka may be found in Kuwait Government Press, 1964, fig. 29.

39. BOWL

Cream slip on buff paste
Hellenistic Period
Seventh to first century B.C.
Height 12 cm.
26°17+'N   50°02+'E

An ancient repair technique is demonstrated here. No evidence of lacing material remains. A small flat foot measures 6.8 cm. in diameter. The closest published parallel is from Ain Jawan, Saudi Arabia (Bowen, 1950, fig. 19).

40a. JUG

Green glaze on a buff paste
Hellenistic Period
Seventh to first century B.C.
Height 24.7 cm.
26°33+'N   50°04+'E

A barely discernible incised rocker pattern, 2 cm. high, encircles the shoulder under the loops formed by the two slightly grooved strap handles. A horizontal row of shallow indentations appears just below the handles. The bottom is finished with a small ringbase. The jug has been glazed on all surfaces with a green glaze that now appears mostly brown. Ghirshman shows a Parthian jug with two handles and a rocker design (Ghirshman, 1962, Pl. 134). A Hellenistic jug of similar shape was excavated at the Greek temple area on Failaka (Kuwait Government Press, 1964, fig. 28).

40b. SMALL BOWL

Gold patina on a beige paste
Hellenistic Period
Seventh to first century B.C.
Height 5 cm.
26°33+'N   50°04+'E

A beautiful gold patina is all that remains of the original glaze on this delicate bowl which has a small ring base. A slight horizontal groove is evident on the exterior two-thirds of the way down the side. The outline of a circle is impressed on the interior bottom.

41a. MINIATURE JAR

Alabaster
Hellenistic Period
Height 6 cm.
26°33+'N   50°04+'E

When new, this flat-bottomed jar had two horizontally-pierced lugs. Doe pictures jars with the same style of pierced lugs from the Muncherjee collection in the Aden Museum (Doe, 1971, Pl. 37 and p. 115). Small alabaster jars of similar shape but with unpierced handles have been excavated in southwest Arabia (Van Beek, 1969, pp. 273, 275, fig. 118b and 119g). See also Cleveland, 1965, Pl. 89 and pp. 110-111.

41b. LARGE BOWL

Red slip on a red paste
Hellenistic Period
Height 14.2 cm.
26°33+'N 50°04+'E

Below the thickened rim are two finger grooves. The bottom is flat and measures ca. 14.5 cm. in diameter. The paste shows specks of pale yellow. The bowl is slipped on all surfaces.

41c. JUG

Green glaze on beige paste
Hellenistic Period
Seventh to first century B.C.
Height 27 cm.
26°33+'N 50°04+'E

The graceful proportions of this jug are enhanced by the beautiful silver patina which shows traces of the original green glaze. A substantial ring base completes the bottom.

42. BEADS

Hellenistic Period
Seventh century B.C. to first century A.D.
25°49+'N 50°03+'E

Agate, lapis lazuli, rock crystal and other beautifully colored stones compliment the carnelian beads from the Hellenistic site called "Gerrha" by local archaeology buffs. Due to the wind erosion of this site hundreds of beads remain on the surface. Potts, et al, 1978, provide an excellent historical account of Gerrha.

43a. JUG

Gold patina on a beige paste
Hellenistic Period
Seventh to first century B.C.
Height 14.3 cm.
26°33+'N 50°04+'E

The beautifully patinated glaze has minute traces of green color. Two incised bands of rocker design on the shoulder are almost obliterated by the glaze. The rim has an inner ledge which provides for a lid. Small handles of this type were very popular from Neo-Babylonian through Persian periods as evidenced by the large number of vessels excavated at Ur (Woolley, 1962, Pl. 56, 57, pp. 99, 100). Ghirshman reports such a jug from Susa and classifies it as Parthian, second to third centuries A.D. (Ghirshman, 1962, Pl. 133). Bibby describes a similar jug with two small handles on the shoulder recovered from a grave on Bahrain. He compares it with the City V Selucid pottery and suggests a date of 300 to 100 B.C. (Bibby, 1969, Pl. XVIII).

43b. SMALL BOWL

Gold patina on a beige paste
Hellenistic Period
Height 5.5 cm.
26°33+'N 50°04+'E

This small bowl was decorated on the lower exterior with a radiating pattern of thick straight lines pressed into the clay somewhat carelessly in few instances. The fluted metal work of the fifth and early fourth centuries B.C. may have inspired the pattern. See an example of this fluting on a metal vase in Porada, 1962, Pl. 49. Hamilton suggests an earlier date, 722-612 B.C. in writing about a fluted silver bowl and its parallels in bronze and clay (Hamilton, 1966, p. 7). Described as a "tulip bowl" by Wheeler, it was a very popular shape at Charsada where examples were found in considerable numbers and dated approximately third to second centuries B.C. (Wheeler, 1962, p. 40 and fig. 10).

43c. BOWL

Cream slip on red paste
Hellenistic Period
Around 300 B.C.
Height 11.8 cm.
26°33+'N 50°04+'E

Two prominent grooves are placed 4.5 cm. below the plain rounded rim which thickens slightly at the top. The lower sides and slightly convex bottom have been shaved rather unevenly. A partial horizontal row of nail impressions is visible on one side of the bowl.

44a. EARRING

Gold
Hellenistic Period
Seventh to first century B.C.
Length 2.8 cm.
26°42+'N 49°57+'E

Fine granulation in a geometric design decorates the hollow ball of this earring. This interesting technique of decoration in gold was known as early as Sumerian times (Hawkes and Woolley, 1963, p. 568). Included in the gold jewelry from Nimrud was a cylindrical gold bead decorated in triangles formed by minute granules. The date suggested is late seventh century B.C. (Curtis and Maxwell-Hyslop, 1971, Pl. XXXa and p. 110).

44b. FIGURINE

Terracotta dove
Cream slip on red paste
Hellenistic Period
Third century B.C. to first century A.D.
Height without head 4.4 cm.
26°52+'N   48°43'E

The small dove, whose head has been restored with plasticene, was found at Thaj. A median line from head to tail divides the body. Oblique lines mark the feathers on each wing. The small pedestal base is slightly concave.

45a. JAR

Cream paste
Hellenistic Period
Third century B.C. to first century A.D.
Height 20 cm.
26°55+'N   49°38+'E

The jar is divided into two sections with the entire design confined to the upper 9 cm. Four horizontal rows of deep crescent thumbnail markings and a row of rocker design are spaced with incised lines so that the narrower bands are closer to the top. The rim is missing. A ring base completes the bottom.

45b. EARRING

Gold
Sassanian Period
Third to seventh century A.D.
Length 2 cm.
26°42+'N   49°57+'E

Ten granulations arranged in two rows compliment a hollow gold ball. See Whitehouse for a pair of earrings in this style excavated at the site of the Great Mosque at Siraf (Whitehouse, 1972, Pl. XIIc).

45c. JUG AND PLATE

Jug: Green glaze on cream paste
Parthian Period
Mid-third century B.C. to mid-third century A.D.
Height 12.3 cm.
Plate: Silver patina on a cream paste
Diameter 27.8 cm.
26°33+'N   50°04+'E

The flat top with the narrow neck, when combined with the small lug handles having a pronounced upper lobe, place this little jug in the Parthian period. A ring base completes the bottom. Tiny specks of green hint at the original color of the glaze. Large plates, similar to this one, were common during this period.

46a. CAMEL HEADS

Red and gray paste
Hellenistic Period
Third century B.C. to first century A.D.
Tallest fragment 6 cm.
26°52+'N 48°43'E

Many animal heads are found at the Selucid sites of Thaj and Al Hinnat. The paste is frequently heavily sand tempered and the figures are often slipped in cream although these examples do not retain any slip. Punctuated designs are common. Frequently the eye is an applied pellet with a deep hole. Nostrils and mouth are usually indicated and sometimes a Wasm (brand) shows on the thigh or neck. An excellent description of this site is furnished by Mandaville, 1963, pp. 9-20. Also see Bibby, 1969, p. 322.

46b. JUG

Patinated glaze on cream paste
Hellenistic Period
Third to first century B.C.
Height 32 cm.
26°33+'N 50°04+'E

A similar jug with a green glaze was found above the City IV floor at Qala'at al-Bahrain by the Danish expedition (Bibby, 1966, fig. 9).

47a. STONE WITH INSCRIPTION

Limestone
Height of fragment 56 cm.
26°56+'N 48°46'E

Found beside a dry well at Al Hinnat, this stone had been reused in the well structure. Grooves cut by ropes are visible on the reverse side.

The inscription is in the South Arabian script. It has been identified as part of a tombstone, but so few characters remain that translation is limited. The western and southern parts of the Arabian Peninsula have numerous such stones but their occurrence in the Eastern Province is rare. For a record of the inscribed stones from Thaj see Mandaville, 1963, pp. 9-20.

47b. SEAL IMPRESSION ON A SHERD

Cream slip on red paste
Hellenistic Period
300 B.C. to 100 A.D.
Length of sherd 11 cm.
Thickness of sherd 2.5 cm.
Diameter of impression 2.6 cm.
26°52+'N 48°43'E

This very large heavy pot from Thaj has a curved row of applied decoration with fingertip impressions. Adams has a comparative collection of seal impressions from Achaemenid through Late Abbasid Periods (Adams, 1965, fig. 16).

206

47c. SEAL IMPRESSIONS ON A RIM SHERD

Cream slip on red paste
Hellenistic Period
300 B.C. to 100 A.D.
Length of rim 19 cm.
Diameter of impression 2.9 cm.
26°52+'N   48°43'E

This heavy thick rim found at Thaj retains part of a second impression spaced 5.5 cm. from the complete one. On the side of the sherd, just below the rim (not visible in the photo) a horizontal row of fingertip impressions decorate the clay. The seal impressions, although badly weathered, appear to be of the same general style as the one in Pl. 47b. Bibby tells us about his examination of Thaj in the spring of 1968 (Bibby, 1969, pp. 365-369).

48. FIGURINES

Hellenistic Period
Third century B.C. to first century A.D.
26°52+'N   48°43'E

Terracotta heads such as these from Thaj are found on seated or squatting female figures with exaggerated breasts. The pudenda are frequently shown in a punctuated triangle. Only one of these pictured here has any naturalistic features. The others seem to be deliberately semi-human. Bibby describes such figures from Thaj (Bibby, 1969, p. 327).

A. *Height 5.4 cm.* This naturalistic face has traces of cream slip on the red paste. The eyes and lips are formed by applied pellets. The chin has a puncture. Two braids depict the hair style.

B. *Height 5.3 cm.* Pelleted eyes, punctuated nostrils, a slash for a mouth, and a row of beads (?) about the neck decorate the red paste of this figurine.

C. *Height 4.8 cm.* The gray paste appears to have been fired in a reducing kiln. The eyes are pelleted. The neck is decorated with both lines and punctuated design.

D. *Height 4.8 cm.* A very stylized head with but a single puncture for an eye and a few slashes for nose, mouth, and neck, is formed out of red paste with considerable sand temper.

49a. JUG

Cream slip on buff paste
Hellenistic Period
300 B.C. to 100 A.D.
Height 34 cm.
Maximum thickness front to back 21.5 cm.
26°15+'N   50°03+'E

This unique flask has its handles pierced perpendicularly to the classical Hellenistic neck. Too large to be carried on a person, too fragile to be carried far on an animal, where a skin bag would be preferable, its use is controversial. The bottom is rounded.

49b. BOWL

    Cream slip on a red paste
    Hellenistic Period
    Third century B.C. to first century A.D.
    Height 5.5 cm.
    26°52+'N 48°42'E

Typical of the Thaj bowls is this thin-walled incurving rim with three horizontal lines. The interior appears gray in sections, probably the result of having been overfired. The lower section and the flat foot have been shaved thin.

50. BRONZE LIONESS

    Sassanian Period
    Third to seventh century A.D.
    Height 3.6 cm.
    26°19'N 50°00+'E

The under section of this petite figurine is crudely finished as though it had been an attached ornament. The ears protrude like little knobs. The front legs separate above the feet. A lovely patina has developed on the surface.

51a. SPINDLE AND WHORLS

    Bone
    Spindle length 15.5 cm.
    Whorls diameter ca. 2.5 cm.
    27°00+'N 49°38+'E

Spinning whorls and bone spindles have been used over a long period and continue to be used even today. The whorls pictured here are flat on one surface and convex on the other. The convex surfaces are frequently decorated with tiny dotted circles. Bibby reports a bone spindle from a Selucid grave on Bahrain (Bibby, 1969, bPl. XVIII).

51b. CAMEL FIGURINE

    Cream slip on red paste
    Hellenistic Period
    Third century B.C. to first century A.D.
    Total length 12.5 cm.
    26°52+'N 48°43'E

This camel body from Thaj is decorated in a rouletted punctuated design which extends from the broken section on the leg along both sides of the hump to the broken neck. Two more vertical rows of markings decorate each side. The legs of these figurines are usually cone shaped. Punctuated markings sometimes indicate the female of the species. Occasionally wasms (brands) are marked on the neck or thigh. Except during mating season the female camel would have the more drooping tail which leads us to suppose that the figurines were connected somehow with the fertility of the herd. Mandaville, one of the early explorers of this area, furnished an excellent report on his observations (Mandaville, 1963, pp. 9-20). Other camel figures with raised and curled tails are engraved into the rock-art in central Arabia (Anati, 1968, Pl. XVI, p. 54, and Pl. XXXIII, Fig. 64, pp. 102, 103).

52a. STORAGE JAR

Red paste
Sassanian Period
Third to seventh centuries A.D.
Height 45.5 cm.
26°33+'N   50°04+'E

This large storage jar, used as a ossuary, was found on Tarut Island. It probably dates to a Zoroastrian settlement during the Sassanian period. A number of these large jars have been recovered from the gardens north of Darin.

52b. JAR

Cream slip on red paste
Sassanian Period
Third to seventh century A.D.
Height 16.8 cm.
27°07+'N   49°29'E

A flat base supports this simple small storage jar. Dating is possible because it was found nested with four other vessels, not pictured here, but which belong in this period.

52c. UTILITARIAN KITCHENWARE

Red paste
Late Islamic
Height 24.5 cm.
26°44+'N   49°44+'E

The coarse red clay with copious sand temper has turned black and grayish in areas exposed to fire. Four knobby handles and an extremely convex bottom were very popular features and are found on many such cookpots here.

53. JUG

Gray paste with copious cream-colored temper
Height 23 cm.
26°50'N   49°31+'E

A single strap handle and two incised lines on the shoulder are the main features of this unglazed jug. Fired in a reducing kiln, the paste appears gray. The ridges, formed by finger-pressure during turning, extend from 2.5 cm. above the concave bottom to 2 cm. below the handle.

54. LARGE BOWL

Blue-green glaze on porous cream paste
Late Sassanian or Early Islamic Period
600 to 800 A.D.
Height ca. 30 cm.
27°14+'N   49°31+'E

Glazed on all surfaces, the heavy carved bowl has a substantial ring base. The deep carving, limited to the area above the carination, is divided into vertical sections. Different arrangements of the same design elements appear in each section. Lane describes this technique as "chip-carved triangular nicks" and tells us that the same blue-green alkaline glaze was used through the Parthian (249 B.C.- A.D. 226) and Sassanian times (A.D. 226-641) and well into the Islamic period (Lane, 1951, pp. 8-9). This style of decoration is not found in the Eastern Province as frequently as that shown in Pl. 57c. Quite possibly the deep carving weakened the vessel making it difficult to transport long distances.

55a. STORAGE JAR

Gray finish on red paste
Sassanian Period
Third to seventh century A.D.
Height 39.2 cm.
26°53+'N   49°37+'E

A unique large storage vessel with a tall straight neck has an almost flat rim which extends into the neck opening. Just below the rim, repeated half way down the neck and again where the neck joins the body, are deep nail prints on a cordon. The carination has a heavy cordon decorated with a zig-zag incised line. The shoulder has another wide zig-zag while the neck has two smaller ones. The lower section of the vessel is missing. The gray finish is the result of reduction firing in the kiln.

55b. JUG

Cream paste
Early Islamic
Tenth century A.D.
Height 14.3 cm.
26°05+'N   49°49'E

The thin walls have been incised by the use of a two-pronged implement which created a double line. The pattern is divided into vertical sections which cover most of the rounded body. Oblique grids are interspaced by vertical wavy lines. A sharp carination placed low on the body provides an unusual shape. A delicate ring base finishes the bottom. The scars for a single handle remain on the shoulder and neck. The rim is missing but deep in the neck a section of a filter remains. See Lane, 1951, Pl. 36, for a similar jug. Variations of this style are reported by Wilkinson, 1976, pp. 336-340.

56a. JUG

Blue-green glaze on a buff paste
Sassanian to Early Islamic
Height 27 cm.
27°00+'N   49°38+'E

At first glance this jug appears coil-made; but a closer examination of the interior bottom contradicts this premise. The glaze extends inside the neck and on the exterior of the ring-base bottom.

56b. JUG

Blue-green glaze on a porous buff paste
Sassanian to Early Islamic Periods
Height 39.5 cm.
26°22'N   50°12+'E

Found upright in the ground, this jug had a gray flat-bottomed bowl fragment inverted over the rim. The glaze drips approximately 5 cm. inside the neck and also covers the ring-base bottom. Where they join the body, the two thick strap handles almost obliterate three incised lines which encircle the rim.

57a. SHALLOW BOWL

Green glaze on molded apricot paste
Islamic Period
Ninth century
Height 3.3 cm.
27°07+'N   49°28'E

Sparingly applied to the exterior bottom, the green glaze is thick and dark on the interior. The repousse pattern repeats itself nine times around the bowl. Oblique lines mark the design into triangles. The lower sections contain a three-leaf arrangement placed on top of a small triangle which is marked with inverted "V's", each with central dot. The upper sections have lines spreading in a fan arrangement connected on the top by a series of small arches. Lane shows several examples of molded ware (Lane, 1951, Pl. 4). The Freer Gallery of Art has a striking flat platter decorated with gold-lustered glaze (Smithsonian Institution, 1960, Pl. 1). A small bowl similar in shape to the Arabian example is pictured in Hobson, 1932, Pl. II fig. 2.

57b. SHALLOW BOWL

Light gray steatite
Islamic Period
Height 5.9 cm.
26°21'N   50°12+'E

A rather carelessly-executed incised design has as its main feature a row of small squares each with a central dotted-circle and diagonal lines extending to the corners. Rectangles, taller than they are wide, interspace these squares. Each rectangle is decorated with a grid of oblique lines. A similar large rectangle reaching from the top to the bottom flanks the small ledge finger grip, half way down one side, which protrudes approximately 3 mm. A lightly scratched zig-zag line, spaced between two deep horizontal lines, appears below and again above the squares. Judging by the design and the ledge handle arrangement, it seems reasonable to place this bowl late in the Islamic Period.

57c. STORAGE JAR

Thick blue-green glaze on porous cream paste
Late Sassanian or Early Islamic
Sixth to eighth century A.D.
Height 67.5 cm.
26°56+'N 49°36+'E

Three small crescent lug handles with deeply incised oblique lines are spaced just below the rim of this storage jar. The design, repeated three times, is formed by a combination of pellets and ribbons of clay applied to the surface. It features a willow-like tree under a large arch. Vertical rows of raised ornamentation in the form of small rosettes separate the three arches. Each rosette, a circle of minute dots around a central raised knob, gives the impression of having been applied with a mold. An incised zig-zag line encircles the jar approximately 27 cm. above the glazed ring base repeating the smaller zig-zag at the rim. A similar jar in the Louvre is pictured by Lane, 1951, Pl. 3. Whitehouse excavated another under the platform of the Great Mosque at Siraf (Whitehouse, 1972, Pl. Xb). A third published example is described by Wilkinson, 1963, Pl. 17. The Arabian jar appears to predate these others if judged by the elaborateness of the design.

58a. BOWL FRAGMENT

Lustre painting on cream paste
Ninth century A.D.
Height of bowl 10.7 cm.
Diameter ca. 29 cm.
27°07+'N 49°29'E

The interior of this lustre-painted fragment has light brown, dark brown, olive green and golden yellow on a gray background. The exterior is limited in design and color, employing only golden yellow and light brown in rather large splashes which may represent leaves. The interior design is divided into sections by the use of fine green lines which repeat the color encircling the rim. One section is a herringbone pattern; another, a rough stipple; and still another appears to be small leaves. The bowl, of pleasing shape, is carefully made and is supported by a large ring base. Rice tells us that the Mesopotamian potters are generally responsible for the early development of lustre painting (Rice, 1965, pp. 40-42). A similar use of leaves is illustrated by Hobson, 1932, fig. 7. Caiger-Smith, 1973, gives an excellent account of the origin of lustre painting in the ninth century in the region of Baghdad.

58b. BOWL FRAGMENT

Lustre painting on cream paste
Early Islamic Period
Ninth century
Diameter ca. 23.5 cm.
27°07+'N 49°29'E

Golden yellow, olive green, and ruby decorate the light gray background of this bowl while a band of ruby encircles the rim and forms the delicate lines dividing the spaces on the interior. The exterior, like the example in Pl. 58a which probably came from the same workshop, is decorated in larger leaves. The Sassanian influence is felt in the design which employs flower stalks, leaves, and small dotted areas enclosed in larger amorphous shapes.

58c. BOWL FRAGMENT

Cobalt blue design, white glaze on buff paste
Islamic Period
Ninth century
Height of bowl 5.5 cm.
Diameter ca. 21.5 cm.
27°02+'N   49°27+'E

Thick white glaze covers the exterior leaving only the bottom of a well-formed ring base exposed. The profile, in a graceful curve, suggests a Chinese influence. A similar bowl from Samarra is pictured by Rice, 1965, Pl. 32, p. 38. This particular style of decoration was found as far away as Nishapur where Wilkinson, 1976, tells us it was an import to that area.

59. SMALL BOTTLES

Glass
Islamic Period

Small glass bottles such as these were probably used for cosmetics, perfumes, etc. Evidence of local glass manufacturing has been substantiated. It is interesting to note that glass is not found at the Hellenistic site of Thaj so that we can quite safely say that its general usage in the Eastern Province postdates the occupating of that site. For a glass bottle similar to No. B see Helod-Tretiak, 1970, p. 227.

A. Eighth or ninth century
Height 5.0 cm.
27°00+'N   49°38+'E

This round-bottomed little container has a very delicate appearance.

B. Ninth or tenth century
Height 4.7 cm.
26°41+'N   49°55+'E

The very thin little bottle has a patina in some areas and a high dimpled bottom.

C. Ninth or tenth century
Height 5.9 cm.
26°54+'N   49°40'E

The small molded bottle is very thick and has a slightly concave bottom. Decoration consists of rings around the neck, circular depressions, and vertical ridges.

D. Tenth century
Height 6.2 cm.
27°01+'N   49°37+'E

Similar to tenth century bottles from Egypt, the thick square bottom is cone-shaped inside.

E. Tenth century
Height 4.1 cm.
26°54+'N   49°40'E

The little square bottle with a broken rim has thick sides.

60a. JAR

Cobalt and blue trim, gray glaze on porous buff paste
Islamic Period
Ninth century
Height 16.5 cm.
26°55+'N 49°39+'E

This jar has been glazed on both interior and exterior with traces remaining on the flat bottom. The three small handles, placed high on the shoulder, are trimmed in blue-green glaze. A series of little cobalt splashes occur on each side of the handles. A cobalt line accents the shoulder. The rim is a gentle flange. This jar was found with the bowls in Plates 60b and 60c.

60b. BOWL

Blue-green trim, gray glaze on buff paste
Islamic Period
Ninth century
Height 11 cm.
26°55+'N 49°39+'E

The straight sides of this bowl have a sharp carination 2 cm. from the bottom where they reduce considerably in size to join a low ring base. Three splashes of blue-green, evenly spaced, are the only decoration. The bowl is glazed on all surfaces. The shape and simplicity of design suggest a Chinese influence.

60c. SHALLOW BOWL

Blue-green and black trim, gray glaze on beige paste
Islamic Period
Ninth century
Height 6.8 cm.
26°55+'N 49°39+'E

Applied over a few black lines are predominate blue-green splashes. The design is confined to the interior although the exterior retains glaze in some sections. An asymmetrical ring base supports the flaring sides. Rosen-Aylon pictures a similar plate in the Louvre (Rosen-Aylon, 1971, p. 207).

61a. BOWL

Blue-green trim, white glaze on cream paste
Islamic Period
Ninth century
Height 7 cm.
26°55+'N 49°39+'E

Bold amorphous spots of blue-green glaze decorate a white background which has weathered considerably. When compared with the others on this plate the popularity of this style is emphasized. A shallow ring base finishes the bottom. All surfaces are glazed.

214

61b. BOWL

Green and black trim, yellow glaze on fine apricot paste
Islamic Period
Ninth century
Height 7.5 cm.
27°07+′N   49°29′E

The delicate bowl with a diagonal black grid on a yellow background has splashes of green in each section. The sides invert a little at the top and terminate in a thin edge. The lower section has a sharp carination where the sides narrow to meet the shallow ring base.

61c. BOWL

Creamy-white glaze on cream paste
Islamic Period
Ninth century
Height 8.5 cm.
26°50′N   49°31+′E

An overglaze, perhaps intended to be transparent, appears white in a few areas but for the most part is cream colored. Oblique splashes of cobalt are alternated with blue-green. The carination, low on the bowl, and the slightly incurving sides create a pleasing effect. Most likely, the Mesopotamia potters were influenced by the T'ang wares (Lane, 1951, pp. 13, 15).

61d. BOWL

Gray glaze on a fine cream paste
Blue-green and black decoration
Islamic Period
Ninth century
Height 9 cm.
26°50′N   49°31+′E

Black leaves (?) are interspaced with blue-green streaks on a solid gray background. The decoration ends at the low carination. All surfaces are glazed.

62a. EAR CLEANER

Bronze
Length 11.5 cm.
27°01′N   49°36+′E

An ear cleaner in the shape of a tiny concave spoon would be a most practical implement in a desert environment. This decorated bronze one is more elaborate than many found here. Two small circles decorate each side of the square base. The reverse side of the spoon has four more circles.

62b. SEAL RING

Black stone set in silver
26°05+'N 49°49'E

A black stone has a clear-cut inscription in Arabic. Intended to be used as a seal, it is set in a heavy silver ring. Translated its read: Mohammad Arfuj the son of Hassan in the year 1137. The 3 is indefinite. This establishes the ring as approximately 250 years old.

62c. APPLICATOR

Mother-of-pearl
Length 6.1 cm.
26°15+'N 50°03'E

A beautiful mother-of-pearl applicator is set in a small bronze cap. Probably it was used as a wand for perfume. It seems a little large, too blunt, and too pretty to have been used to apply khol, the popular black eye make-up.

63a. LARGE JAR

Blue-green glaze on cream paste
Islamic Period
Twelfth century
Height 52 cm.
Purchased in Hofuf

Only two of the original four small lug handles remain. The light blue-green glaze which ends just above the ring base has some vertical streaks where the glaze is slightly thicker and darker.

63b. STORAGE JAR

Buff paste
Late Islamic
Height 51 cm.
26°49+'N 49°59+'E

A flat rim 2.5 cm. wide extends inward on this large jar which has a deliberate hole in the center of the bottom. Added to the buff paste is a white temper.

64a. JUG

Cream slip on red paste
Islamic Period
First half of eighteenth century
Height 17.5 cm.
25°28+'N 49°33+'E

A single handle on this small-footed jug helps create the feeling of imbalance. Vessels of this same distinctive shape, influenced by Turkish and South Arabian pottery, were recovered from a shipwreck in the Red Sea (Raben, 1971, pp. 146-155).

216

64b. LAMP

Blue-green glaze on cream paste
Height 2.3 cm.
27°14+'N   49°31+'E

Remarkable in their absence from this area are the terracotta lamps which are so popular in adjacent regions. This rare example comes from a site that appears almost entirely Sassanian from surface debris. Wilkinson, 1974, pp. 233, 234 and 245, describes a variety of lamps from Nishapur.

64c. COOKPOT

Cream slip on red paste
Late Islamic Period
Seventeenth or eighteenth century
Height 16.5 cm.
27°27+'N   49°16+'E

A late Islamic handmade cookpot with a wide-ridged rim has a round bottom. Gravel tempering shows in the porous paste. It was found together with a similar vessel badly burned on the bottom. In the same group was a small bowl and a lid with a knob handle which was fashioned from a light paste.

65. BRACELET FRAGMENTS

Glass
Late Islamic Period

Glass bracelets appear to have been worn as recently as the turn of the century. The earliest found here (plain black) have come from a site associated with sixteenth century Ming pottery. Some bracelets are very small with an inside diameter no larger than 4.7 cm., perhaps fashioned for children, although today's Arab women are noticeably small of stature.

66a. QUERN STONES

Islamic Period
Diameter ca. 31 cm.
26°44+'N   49°55+'E

Querns such as these are frequently found at Islamic sites. The two stones, placed with the flat side together on a skin or cloth, have a dowel inserted in the central hole to keep them aligned. The upper stone is then turned by the use of a stick in the small off-center opening. As grain is poured through the top, the flour which spills over the edge is caught on the skin. Bread made with such flour usually contains so much fine sand that it is damaging to the teeth if eaten for extended periods. One of these stones is fashioned from limestone; the other, from a dark colored conglomerate.

66b. PEARLING WEIGHTS, LOOM/NET WEIGHTS

Pearling weights: stone
Islamic Period
Length of largest weight 19 cm.
Weight ca. 4.1 kg.
26°49+'N   49°59+'E

The three large weights, each with a hole, are smooth, extremely heavy for their size, and display rope burns from usage over a long period of time. It is highly probable that they were employed as pearling weights worn about the divers' necks to enable them to descend rapidly. All three have been fashioned from a stone with a sparking metallic luster.

Loom/net weights:

Islamic Period

The smaller stones, usually classified as loom/net weights, are frequently found around ancient habitation sites. Sometimes they are made from clay or fashioned from broken pottery. Likewise small stones with drilled holes are also utilized. At Charsada Wheeler excavated a cart which had wheels fashioned from clay (Wheeler, 1962, Pl. XXXV, XXXVI).

67. BOWL

Light gray steatite
Late Islamic Period
Height 11.2 cm.
27°27+'N   49°18'E

This bowl was mended in antiquity with strips of copper inserted through the tiny holes and twisted together on the exterior. Seven such strips remain intact. Six additional holes remain. The ledge handles protrude 1.0 cm. The flat bottom which is badly desintegrated appears to have been used over a fire.

BIBLIOGRAPHY

ADAMS, ROBERT McC.
1965   *Land Behind Baghdad,* Chicago: University of Chicago Press.

ADAMS, ROBERT McC. AND HANS J. NISSEN
            The Uruk Countryside, Chicago: University of Chicago Press.

ADAMS, ROBERT McC. AND PETER J. PARR, MUHAMMAD IBRAHIM,
    ALI S. AL-MUGHANNUM
1977   Saudi Arabian Archaeological Reconnaissance 1976, *Atlal* Vol. 1, Riyadh: Department of
            Antiquities and Museums.

ANATI, E.
1968   *Rock-Art in Central Arabia* Vol. 1, The Oval-Headed People of Arabia, Louvain: Institute
            Orientaliste, University of Louvain.
            Rock-Art in Central Arabia Vol. 2, Part One, The Fat-Tailed Sheep in Arabia, Part Two,
            The Realistic-Dynamic Style of Rock-Art in the Jebel Qara, Louvain: Institute Orientaliste,
            University of Louvain.

BIBBY, GEOFFREY
1964   Arabiens Arkaeologi, *Kuml,* Copenhagen: Jutland Archaeological Society.
1966   Arabiens Arkaeologi, *Kuml,* Copenhagen: Jutland Archaeological Society.
1969   *Looking for Dilmum,* New York: Alfred A. Knopf.
1973   *Preliminary Survey in East Arabia 1968,* Copenhagen: Jutland Archaeological Society.

BOWEN, RICHARD LeBARON, JR.
1950   The Early Arabian Necropolis of Ain Jawan, *Bulletin of the American Schools of
            Oriental Research,* New Haven: American Schools of Oriental Research.

BURKHOLDER, GRACE
1971   Steatite Carvings from Saudi Arabia, *Artibus Asiae* XXXIII, 4, Ascona: Institute of Fine
            Arts, New York University.
1972   Ubaid Sites and Pottery in Saudi Arabia, *Archaeology* 25, No. 4, New York:
            Archaeological Institute of America.

BURKHOLDER, GRACE AND MARNY GOLDING
1971   Surface Survey of Al-'Ubaid Sites in the Eastern Province, *Contributions to the
            Anthropology of Saudi Arabia,* Miami: Field Research Projects.

BURNEY, C.A.
1961   Excavations at Yanik Tepe, Iran, *Iraq* XXIII, 2, London: British School of Archaeology
            in Iraq.
1962   Excavations at Yanik Tepe, Azerbiajan, 1961, Second Preliminary Report, *Iraq* XXIV, 2,
            London: British School of Archaeology in Iraq.

CAIGER-SMITH, ALAN
1973   *Tin Glaze Pottery in Europe and the Islamic World,* London: Faber and Faber.

CLEVELAND, RAY L.
1965   *An Ancient South Arabian Necropolis, Objects from the Second Campaign (1951) in Timna' Cemetery,* Baltimore: The John Hopkins Press.

CORNWALL, P.B.
1946   Ancient Arabia: Explorations in Hasa 1940-41, *Geographical Journal* CVII, No. 1 and 2.

CURTIS, J.E. AND K.R. MAXWELL-HYSLOP
1971   The Gold Jewellry from Nimrud, *Iraq* XXXIII, 2, London: The British School of Archaeology in Iraq.

DANIEL, GLYN
1968   *The First Civilizations,* New York: Thomas Y. Crowell Co.

DELAUGAZ, PINHAS
1952   *Pottery from the Diyala Region,* Chicago: University of Chicago Press.

DICKSON, H.R.P.
1949   *The Arab of the Desert,* London, George Allen and Unwin Ltd.

DOE, BRIAN
1971   *Southern Arabia,* London: Thames and Hudson.

DURRANI, F.A.
1964   Stone Vases as Evidence of Connection Between Mesopotamia and the Indus Valley, *Ancient Pakistan* I.

DuRY, CAREL J.
1969   *Art of the Ancient and Near Middle East,* New York, London: Harry N. Abrams, Inc.

FIELD, HENRY
1958   Stone Implements from the Rub' al-Khali, Southern Arabia, *Man* Vol. LVIII.
1971   *Contributions to the Anthropology of Saudi Arabia,* Miami: Field Research Projects.

FRANKFORT, HENRI
1935   *Oriental Institute Discoveries in Iraq, 1933/34,* Chicago: University of Chicago Press.

FRIFELT, KAREN
1970   Jamdat Nasr Graves in Oman, *Kuml,* Arhus: Jutland Archaeological Society.
1971   Excavations in Abu Dhabi (Oman), *Artibus Asiae* XXXIII, 4, Ascona: Institute of Fine Arts, New York University.

GIRSHMAN, ROMAN
1962   *Persian Art,* New York: Golden Press.

HAMILTON, R.W.
1966   A Silver Bowl in the Ashmolean Museum, *Iraq* XXVIII, 1, London: British School of Archaeology in Iraq.

HARRISON, DAVID L.
1972   *The Mammals of Arabia* Vol. III, London: Ernest Benn Ltd.

HAWKES, JACQUETTA, AND SIR LEONARD WOOLLEY.
1963   *History of Mankind, Vol. 1, Prehistory and the Beginnings of Civilization,* New York: Harper and Row.

HOBSON, R.L.
1932   *A Guide to the Islamic Pottery of the Near East,* London: British Museum.

HOLOD-TRETIAK, RENATA
1970   Qasr al-Hayr al Sharqi, *Archaeology* 23, No. 3, New York: Archaeological Institute of America.

KAPEL, HOLGER
1964   Stone-Age Discoveries in Qatar, *Kuml,* Arhus: Jutland Archaeological Society.
1967   *Atlas of the Stone-Age Cultures of Qatar,* Arhus: Jutland Archaeological Society.
1973   Stone-Age Survey, *Preliminary Survey in East Arabia, 1968,* Arhus: Jutland Archaeological Society.

KHAN, F.A.
1964   *Indus Valley and Early Iran,* Karachi: Department of Archaeology and Museums.

LAMBERG-KARLOVSKI, C.C.
1970   *Excavations at Tepe Yahya, Iran,* Cambridge: American School of Prehistoric Research, and Shiraz: The Asia Institute of Pahlavi University.
1972   Tepe Yahya 1971, Mesopotamia and the Indo-Iranian Borderland, *Iran* Vol. X, London: The British Institute of Persian Studies.

LANE, ARTHUR
1951   *Early Islamic Pottery,* London: Faber and Faber.

LEAKY, RICHARD L. AND ROGER LEWIN
1978   *People of the Lake,* Garden City: Anchor Press/Doubleday.

LINTON, DAVID
1961   Aerial Aid to Archaeology, *Natural History* LXX, No. 12, New York: American Museum of Natural History.

MALLOWAN, M.E.L.
1965   *Early Mesopotamia and Iran,* New York: McGraw-Hill Book Co.
1967   *The Development of Cities from Al 'Ubaid to the End of Uruk 5,* Part 1, Cambridge: Cambridge University Press.

MANDAVILLE, JAMES P.
1963   Thaj: A Pre-Islamic Site in Northeastern Arabia, *Bulletin of the American Schools of Oriental Research* No. 172, Jerusalem and Baghdad: American Schools of Oriental Research.

MASRY, ABDULLAH H.

1974   *Prehistory in Northeastern Arabia: The Problems of Interregional Interaction,* Miami: Field Research Projects.

1977   The Historic Legacy of Saudi Arabia. *Atlal* Vol. 1, Riyadh: Department of Antiquities and Museums.

McCLURE, HAROLD

1971   *The Arabian Peninsula and Prehistoric Populations,* Miami: Field Research Projects.

1978   Ar Rub' Al Khali, *Quaternary Period in Saudi Arabia,* Edited by Saad S. Al-Sayari and Josef G. Zotl, New York: Springer-Verlag.

1978   Radiocarbon Chronology of Late Quaternary Lakes in The Arabian Desert, *Nature* Vol. 263.

MINISTRY OF GUIDANCE AND INFORMATION

1964   *Archaeological Investigations in the Island of Failaka 1958-1964,* Kuwait: Kuwait Government Press.

MORTENSEN, PEDER

1970   Om Barbartemplets Datering, *Kuml,* Arhus: Jutland Archaeological Society.

OATES, DAVID AND JOAN OATES

1976   *The Rise of Civilization,* New York: E.P. Dutton and Co.

OATES, JOAN

1976   Prehistory in Northeastern Arabia, *Antiquity* L.

OATES, JOAN AND T.E. DAVIDSON, D. KAMILLI, H. McKERELL

1977   Seafaring Merchants of Ur?, *Antiquity* LI.

PERKINS, ANN

1949   *The Comparative Archaeology of Mesopotamia,* Chicago: University of Chicago Press.

PORADA, EDITH

1962   *Art of the World, Ancient Iran,* London: Methuen.

1965   Relative Chronology of Mesopotamia: I, *Chronologies in Old World Archaeology,* Chicago and London: University of Chicago Press.

1971   Remarks on Seals Found in the Gulf States, *Atribus Asiae* XXXIII, 4, Ascona: Institute of Fine Arts, New York University.

1971   Some Results of the Third International Conference on Asian Archaeology in Bahrain, March 1970: New Discoveries in the Persian/Arabian Gulf States and Relations with Artifacts from Countries of the Ancient Near East, Introductory Remarks, *Artibus Asiae* XXXIII, 4, Ascona: Institute of Fine Arts, New York University.

POTTS, DANIEL AND 'ALI S. MUGHANNUM, JEFFREY FRYE, DONALD SANDERS

1978   Comprehensive Archaeological Survey Program, Preliminary Report on the Second Phase of the Eastern Province Survey 1397/1977, *Atlal* Vol. 2, Riyadh: Department Of Antiquities and Museums.

RABEN, AVNER
1971   The Shipwreck off Sharm-el-Sheikh, *Archaeology* 24, No. 2, New York: Archaeological
            Institute of America.

RICE, DAVID TALBOT
1965   *Islamic Art,* New York: Frederick A. Praeger.

ROSEN-AYALON, MYRIAM
1971   Islamic Pottery from Susa, *Archaeology* 24, No. 3, New York: Archaeological Institute of
            America.

SMITHSONIAN INSTITUTION
1960   *Medieval Near Eastern Ceramics,* Washington.
1962   *Ancient Glass in the Freer Gallery of Art,* Washington.

SORDINAS, AGUSTUS
1973   *Contributions to the Prehistory of Saudi Arabia* Vol. II, Miami: Field Research Projects.
1978   *Contributions to the Prehistory of Saudi Arabia* Vol. III, Miami: Field Research
            Projects.

STROMMENGER, EVA
1964   *5000 Years of the Art of Mesopotamia,* New York: Harry N. Abrams.

VAN BEEK, GUS W.
1960   Frankincense and Myrrh, *The Biblical Archaeologist,* Jerusalem and Baghdad: The
            American Schools of Oriental Research.
1969   *Hajar Bin Humeid, Investigations at a Pre-Islamic Site in South Arabia,* Baltimore: The
            John Hopkins Press.

WHEELER, SIR MORTIMER
1962   *Charsada,* London: Oxford University Press.

WHITEHOUSE, DAVID
1972   Excavations at Siraf: Fifth Interim Report, *Iran* X, London: The British Institute of
            Persian Studies.

WHITEHOUSE, DAVID AND ANDREW WILLIAMSON
1973   Sassanian Maritime Trade, *Iran* XI, London: The British Institute of Persian Studies.

WILKINSON, CHARLES K.
1963   *Iranian Ceramics,* New York: Harry N. Abrams.
1974   *Nishapur, Pottery of the Early Islamic Period,* New York: The Metropolitan Museum of
            Art.

WOOLLEY, SIR LEONARD
1934   *Ur Excavations Vol. II, The Royal Cemetery,* London: The British Museum, and
            Philadelphia: Museum of the University of Pennsylvania.
1956   *Ur Excavations Vol. IV, The Early Periods,* London: The British Museum, and
            Philadelphia: Museum of the University of Pennsylvania.
1962   *Ur Excavations Vol. IX, The Neo-Babylonian and Persian Periods,* London: The British
            Museum, and Philadelphia: Museum of the University of Pennsylvania.

ZARINS, JURIS
1978   Typological Studies in Saudi Arabian Archaeology, Steatite Vessels in the Riyadh Museum, *Atlal* Vol. 2, Riyadh: Department of Antiquities and Museums.

ZARINS, JURIS AND MOHAMMAD IBRAHIM, DANIEL POTTS, CHRISTOPHER EDENS
1979   Saudi Arabian Archaeological Reconnaissance 1978, The Preliminary Report on the Third Phase of the Comprehensive Archaeological Survey Program — The Central Province, *Atlal* Vol. 3, Riyadh: The Department of Antiquities and Museums.